MW00595726

POCKET GUIDE TO
ASTROLOGY

ALAN OKEN

The Crossing Press

The Crossing Press
www.crossingpress.com

A division of Ten Speed Press
P.O. Box 7123
Berkeley, California 94707
www.tenspeed.com

ISBN 0-89594-820-6

Cover illustration and design by Tara M. Eoff
Text drawings of the signs by Cynthia Baxter

First printing, 1996
Printed in the U.S.A.

2 3 4 5 6 7 8 9 10—06 05 04 03 02

Dedicated to my dear friend and apprentice, Vance Lesauskis, whose support and hard work helped to make this book possible.

CONTENTS

What Is Astrology?

Human beings are in a very interesting place in the cosmic scheme of things. Our physical bodies have the same needs as those of other mammals. We must have food, shelter, and warmth to survive. But unlike other warm-blooded creatures, we also require a sense of spiritual connection to the larger universe of which we are a part.

Astrology and agriculture were the first sciences. In fact, in most early civilizations (and in many modern ones as well), these two essential elements of human life are totally integrated. The study of the positions of the planets, the Sun, and the Moon as they relate to the great climactic cycles of nature is fundamental to physical existence. But is this earthy application of the heavenly lore the limits of the meaning that the planets hold for us? Is our awareness of the heavens and our solar system only there to satisfy our physical hunger? What about our emotional, mental, and spiritual yearnings?

Humankind has to look upward in order to measure the timing of planting and harvesting. But humankind also has to look inward to understand its own cycles of becoming, its own patterns of growth, its own methods of sowing and reaping the rewards of psychological and spiritual evolution. Astrology brings unity and meaning to the vital relationship between the cultivation of the earth and the cultivation of ourselves.

The planets and stars in the heavens above, and our little lives here on this, the third revolving globe outwards from the Sun, have an inseparable linkage: all is One in the Cosmos. Astrology serves as a way to see this fundamental interconnectedness and the beautiful unity of all life. Over many centuries, astrology has developed into a system of thought and a way of explaining the seemingly unexplainable chaos of life. Astrology is ancient. We astrologers have complete and accurate horoscopes that were written down on clay tablets as early as 3,000 B.C. This means that astrology was an established study, a written code of understanding, more than 5,000 years ago.

Astrology has its own languages. First and most importantly, it has a symbolic language. This consists of the glyphs that you will see throughout this book. Astrologers can read a great deal into these symbols and the patterns they make, especially when these astrological glyphs are grouped in the form of a map of the heavens for the date, time, and place of your birth. This map is called a "horoscope," and through its understanding, an astrologer can see so much about a person's nature, character, and destiny.

Astrology also has a technical language that relates to the ways in which a horoscope is calculated and interpreted. The language of the horoscope is complex, but we will briefly discuss some of its fundamentals in "The Astrologer and Your Horoscope." A glossary of terms is available in "An Astrological Glossary." If you are interested in studying how to read and interpret an astrological chart, you will find references at the end of this book.

Astrology is as complex as the life it seeks to represent. In this respect, astrology has a number of fields and branches. These are areas of application that many astrologers make into their specialties. Some astrologers have an understanding of all of these various branches and use them without specializing in any one of them, much like an M.D. who is a general practitioner.

Following are the primary areas of astrological study and interest:

1. *Natal astrology*—This is the best-known and most popular form of astrological work. It deals with the calculation and interpretation of a person's horoscope or birth chart. Natal astrology can be divided into two major orientations:

   a. *exoteric*—This is the study of our ordinary life: relationships, career, family, health, home, and so on. It also includes the psychological approach to life found in the majority of modern astrology.

   b. *esoteric*—This is the more spiritual area of astrology, dealing with the life of the Soul. Esoteric astrology addresses karma, reincarnation, spiritual purpose, and much more.

2. *Mundane astrology*—Countries as well as people are born, have life spans, and die. This can be seen by the recent "death" of the USSR and the births of the numerous former Soviet Republics, for example. We can also see this in the break-up of Yugoslavia and the terrible bloody births of its separate nations. The United States of America was born on July 4, 1776, and there is a horoscope for this event. Through the birth charts of these various nations, the astrologer can view the characteristics and life tendencies for these countries. Mundane astrology also deals in a more general way with national and international politics.

3. *Natural or meteorological astrology*—This branch of astrology is used to forecast earthquakes, weather patterns, and other natural phenomena.

4. *Medical astrology*—As each of the signs and planets relates to certain parts of the body (as well as to various physical states, illnesses, etc.), the trained

medical astrologer can locate the weakest as well as the strongest areas of a person's health. Medicinal herbs are also characterized according to astrological factors, as are all synthetic medicines and drugs.

5. *Electional or horary astrology*—These are the areas of astrology that seek to determine the correct time to begin a particular plan or project. Electional astrology answers such questions as: "When is it the right time to seek a new job?" "Is this a good time for me to invest in the stock market?" "When is the right time for marriage?" Horary work tends to be specific in its use of time. It casts a horoscope and gives an answer from the time the question is actually asked. Horary work has its own set of astrological rules and requires great skill.

In addition to these main areas of study, there are highly developed astrological systems created by other cultures that are beyond the scope of this introductory book. The Hindus, Mayans, Aztecs, Tibetans, Arabs, Hebrews, Egyptians, and Chinese all created highly advanced systems of astrology that are still in use today. The astrological techniques employed by this author and most other modern astrologers in the Western world represent a synthesis of Hebrew, Egyptian, Arabic, Greek, and Roman contributions.

The twentieth century, however, may be considered a period of astrological renaissance. Contemporary astrologers have incorporated a great deal of psychological interpretation into our work, especially the ideas and concepts of psychologist Carl Jung. The amazing advances in computer technology have also permitted astrologers to launch very comprehensive research projects into the mysteries of human nature. Computers, the Internet, e-mail, faxes, and other forms of instant communication enable tens of thousands of professional astrologers and other interested students to be in constant touch with one another, sharing and blending the work that we do. The result of these efforts are often presented through talks and papers at frequent regional, national, and international astrological conferences. Two of the most recent of these were held in Monterey, California, in April of 1995, and in Lucerne, Switzerland, in May of 1996, when at both locations, astrologers from more than thirty countries came together to exchange insights and interests. Astrology evolves its techniques and the application it holds for our lives as we develop and expand our consciousness. Astrology is a living body of knowledge. An understanding of this ancient tool can bring greater joy and creative possibilities into our lives.

The Astrologer and Your Horoscope

Astrology is based an an ancient truth, "As above, so below," as things are in the heavens, so they are here on the Earth. Astrologers look at the positions of the Sun, Moon, and the planets and relate these celestial movements and relationships to earthly events. Astrologers do not think so much in terms of the planets causing things to happen. We look at the planetary indications much more as hands on a giant cosmic clock, pointing to certain circumstances and timing their occurrences.

Each one of us is a reflection of a particular moment in time—the time of our birth. An astrologer can draw a map of the heavens of that special instant and then interpret the positions of the heavenly bodies relative to your character and destiny. Neither character nor destiny have to be 100 percent fated, nor are they etched in cosmic stone, so to speak. As we develop our creative skills and sense of self-awareness, we evolve our ability to make conscious choices. These decisions then work to shape our character and determine our destiny.

The astrologer's primary tool to see and understand a person is contained within the map mentioned above. This is called a "natal horoscope," two words meaning literally "a look (scope) at the hour (horo) of birth (natal)." The *Pocket Guide to Astrology* contains information about three of the most important factors in an astrologer's ability to read a chart: the twelve astrological signs, the planets of the solar system, and the twelve houses (or divisions) of the natal horoscope. After you look at these essential astrological ingredients, you will have a much broader idea as to how this beautiful and ancient science of astrology can work.

The purpose of seeing an astrologer is to get a broader and more objective understanding about yourself and certain major events in your life. Through the various branches of astrology discussed in the previous chapter, the astrologer can share an incredible amount of insights with you. In terms of your basic character and personality, the astrologer can show you what path in life is natural for you. What is a natural personality characteristic to you may not necessarily be what is either best for you or what you wish for yourself. For example, a person may be holding himself back from career advancement because of fears and self-doubt. The trained astrologer can see these natural indications from the positions of the planets in the birth chart. The horoscope may also reveal how such an individual may work to transmute this negative self-image into a more positive one. The professional astrologer can then serve to bring such a reorientation about through carefully explaining the astrological patterns in the horoscope and working in close communication with the client.

The astrologer is able to do this through his or her understanding of how planetary and human life energy work. The horoscope almost always shows alternative "routes": other means and possibilities a person can use to achieve his or her goals in life. You have to be willing to do the necessary work on yourself. But this work is made much easier through a more profound awareness of yourself, and astrology gives you this awareness.

Unless otherwise educated, an astrologer is neither a psychiatrist nor a medical doctor. When a highly trained astrologer comes in contact with a client with severe mental, emotional, or psychological problems, the astrologer always recommends other types of healing. An expert astrologer is gifted, however, in his sense of cycles, the timing of events, and most importantly, in his understanding of human nature.

In this respect, an astrologer will know when it is the best time to get married, when it is appropriate to buy a house, when an investment will yield the best results, if a vacation should be long or short, whom to work with on a group project, whom to hire for a special job, what the best type of education would be for the new child or grandchild in the family, what a person's creative or spiritual potential is all about, and much, much more. In addition, the astrologer will be able to listen to a person with compassion and insight, offering advice and counselling that are in accordance with universal laws.

A prospective astrological client would benefit most from a reading by preparing in the following ways:

1. Do some background reading about astrology so that the astrologer's language is not entirely foreign.
2. If you are totally unfamiliar with the astrologer, ask her how long she has been practicing, where she studied, and if she belongs to any professional astrological organizations. There are several very noteworthy professional groups that work hard to safeguard a high level of astrological practice, and whose members are serious students of astrology. These groups are: the Association for Astrological Networking (AFAN), the International Society for Astrological Research (ISAR), and the National Council for Geocosmic Research (NCGR).
3. Prepare yourself for the consultation. You can do this by bringing along some carefully thought-out questions and issues about which you would like

some information. Try to arrive with an open mind about yourself or the other people you may be interested in better understanding.

4. Make sure that you tape-record your session for future reference. A good reading will be worth listening to again and again, as it will contain a wealth of important information for you. Try not to take notes during the reading (let the tape recorder do that for you). This is better both for you and for the astrologer, as you will then have each other's complete attention.

5. If something is unclear to you, ask the astrologer to explain. Sometimes without meaning to confuse a client, an astrologer may use a technical word or phrase that makes perfect sense to her but no sense to a client untrained in astrological jargon. Perhaps after reading and working with the rest of the *Pocket Guide to Astrology*, you and the astrologer will have much more of this special language in common!

Although it is not the purpose of this book to present a complete guide to the interpretation of a natal chart, you might find it interesting to have a look at such a birth map after it has been calculated and erected. To give you some idea of how such a chart is then worked out and explained, I've included two charts and interpretations in in the chapter "Interpreting the Horoscope." In the meantime, here is the horoscope of the author:

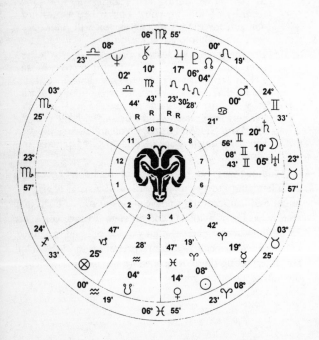

Alan Oken
Tuesday, March 28, 1944 23:04:30
Bronx, New York
Time Zone: 04:00 (EWT)
Longitude 073° W 52' 12"
Latitude 40° N 50' 36"

Calculations by Halloran Software, Los Angeles, California

16

The Planets

Practically all of us are familiar with our Sun Sign and know if we are a Leo or a Taurus or a Gemini. But do we understand what the Sun means when it is not in any of the signs at all? In addition to the Sun, your horoscope of birth contains the zodiacal positions of the Moon, plus all of the other planets in our solar system.

The planets are the power of your chart. We could say that a planet stands for the "what" of the horoscope. What energy or power is at work here? The signs indicate the "how" of your chart. How is this energy moving through your life? How is it affecting you and others through you? The houses of the horoscope give us an understanding of "where." Where in your life, in which part of your daily activities, will the planetary forces take root and play out their celestial role? The chapters "The Twelve Signs of the Zodiac" and "The Houses" speak to us about the "hows" and the "wheres" of your experiences on this planet. Now we shall look more closely at the planets, a word with origins in the language of the ancient Greeks. "Planets" really means "wanderers," as these celestial globes "wander" about as they orbit the Sun. An understanding of the meanings of the planets will reveal to you a great deal about the people and events that wander in and out of your life.

When an astrologer looks at your horoscope, he or she examines the placement of the planets in their various signs. Like the signs, each of the planets (astrologers use this term for the Sun and Moon as well) has a special meaning and significance. An understanding of the three basic elements of astrology—the signs, the houses, and the planets—is essential. Here then are the principal meanings of all the planets commonly used in astrology, followed by a list of planetary associations as they relate to life here on Earth.

All of the celestial bodies mentioned are commonly used by astrologers in their work. However, Hindu astrologers generally do not use Uranus, Neptune, and Pluto in their work. A number of astrologers use several other planets in their astrological work. These include Vulcan, said to orbit between the Sun and Mercury; Transpluto, said to orbit beyond Pluto; and Chiron, a small globe orbiting between Saturn and Uranus. Some astrologers also use four of the largest asteroids in their interpretations of celestial effects. These four are Juno, Vesta, Ceres, and Pallas.

There are two other major points in a chart that are used by all astrologers (especially the Hindus). These are not planets but are so prevalent in astrology that they ought to be mentioned. They are called the "Nodes of the Moon." These two points are determined by the placement of the Moon in the zodiac as it crosses the Earth's orbit in space. The Northern Node tells us about the nature of a person's social contacts and activities. These interchanges are usually very fortunate and advance a person in life. The Southern Node tells us in effect not to waste our energy. It describes the kinds of relationships we may have that no longer serve our best interests and advises us not to pursue these any longer. The positions of all of the planets as well as the Moon's Nodes may be found in an ephemeris (see "An Astrological Glossary"). There is also an ephemeris exclusively for the major asteroids.

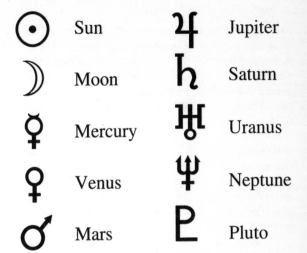

⊙ Sun

☽ Moon

☿ Mercury

♀ Venus

♂ Mars

♃ Jupiter

♄ Saturn

♅ Uranus

♆ Neptune

♇ Pluto

THE SUN

Everything in the Universe is energy. This universal energy is focused in our solar system through the Sun. The Sun is to a person what the nucleus is to an atom: it is the electro-magnetic center of life. Everything within the atom revolves around the nucleus. In the same way everything that is a part of your life, and all of your life potential, is centered in the Sun.

We can say that the Sun represents your individuality. It is the coordinating force that integrates all your various character traits and gives you a sense of your own whole-ness. The Sun is also your "will to be," your urge for life, and the generator of your physical vitality. If you can tap the potential contained within the Sun, you have an unlimited supply of stamina and creativity.

The astrological sign most closely associated with the Sun is Leo the Lion. Leos personify the basic creative urge within us. This is why Leo is the sign so closely related to our creative outpourings. It is especially linked to the arts, dominating the theater and the acting profession. An actor has to be larger than life and project his vitality out into the audience so that every-one can relate to the role he is portraying. Sometimes Leos are larger than life and tend to overly dramatize themselves, dom-inating their social context. But this is only natural as the Lion is ruled by the Sun. As we are all children of the Sun, astrology places an emphasis upon the relationship of Leo and the Sun to young people. Youth is filled with solar vitality and creative potentiality. The legendary "Fountain of Youth" is actually found in the Sun. A truly solar person is always youthful.

In your physical body, the Sun represents the heart and is also concerned with growth and your general health. A strong Sun in a natal chart usually indicates an abundance of physical vigor and vitality, while a weakly placed Sun in the natal chart indicates a person who may easily suffer from low energy levels. Determining the relative strength or weakness of the Sun or any other planet in a horoscope requires either continued studies in astrology on your part or consultation with a professional astrologer.

The Sun's Associations

Sign rulership: Leo
Gemstones: Ruby, hyacinth
Metal: Gold
Day of the week: Sunday
Colors: Orange, yellow-brown, golden shades, deep hues of yellow
Plants, herbs, and flowers: Almond, celandine, chamomile, citrus, frankincense, juniper, marigold, mistletoe, olive, rice, rosemary
Parts of the body: Heart, spleen, anterior pituitary gland
Psychological principle: Basic identity; individuality
Psychological dynamics and keywords:
 positive—self-awareness, individuality, vitality, creativity, courage
 negative—egotism, separatism, domineering, vain, self-centered
Psychological attributes: Source of creative energy, life-force, essence, power, vitality, will, and purpose
Areas of interest: Positions of authority, art, children
Spiritual principles: God the Father, Spirit, Life-giver

THE MOON

The Moon in astrology represents all that is receptive and female. The Moon nourishes and births. She represents our mother and is thus symbolic of that source of our emotional support in life. The Moon also has a great deal to do with our instinctive nature, our biological roots, and our subconscious. She is very involved with dreams, fears, and all emotions. The Moon speaks to us about the cycles of life and especially the female reproductive cycle. When she is positive in a chart, she gives material abundance and emotional strength. She is Mother Nature nourishing her earthly children. When she is negative and poorly placed in a chart, she gives a wild and undisciplined imagination, self-doubt, and a distinct sense of emotional insecurity. In effect, the Moon tells us that life is either a safe and supportive place for us or a deep emotional challenge.

The Moon is most closely linked to the sign Cancer. As such, she represents all that is domestic in our lives. In addition to our mother, the Moon indicates our family life in general and our relationships within the home. I like to refer to the Moon as the vehicle for our "biological karma," as she is so closely connected with our genes, ancestors, and our ties to our particular ethnic origins and traditions.

The Moon's Associations

Sign rulership: Cancer

Gemstones: Moonstone, pearls, crystals

Metals: Silver, aluminum

Day of the week: Monday

Colors: Silvery-grey, opalescent and iridescent hues, white

Plants, herbs, and flowers: Cabbage, clary, coralwort, cucumber, gourd, hyssop, iris, lettuce, melons, moonwort, mushrooms, pearlwort, pumpkin, rosemary, seaweed, watercress, water lily, white rose, willow, wintergreen

Parts of the body: Stomach, uterus, chest, breasts, ovaries

Psychological principle: Emotions, the subconscious

Psychological dynamics and keywords:
    positive—intuitive, sensitive, nurturing, maternal
    negative—dependent, needy, selfish, greedy, moody,
            fearful

Psychological attributes: Feelings, receptivity, moods, security, habits, instincts

Areas of interest: Nursing, child-care, sewing, agriculture, home-care

Spiritual principles: God the Mother, Mother Nature

MERCURY

Mercury represents the rational mind and is very much involved with communication and all the intellectual powers and abilities we may have. Mercury brings to us the urge for knowledge and stimulates life experiences. Mercury keeps us moving from person to person, idea to idea, and place to place. If Mercury is too powerful an influence, it usually creates nervousness and restlessness. It is Mercury you hear as that chatty monkey inside your head, that inner voice that is more of an annoyance than an inspiration!

On the other hand, when Mercury is "under control," then a person has a mind that is stable and reliable, one that gives forth just the right amount of information at just the right time. Mercury is the rational mind, that special gift particular to humanity, allowing us the opportunity to be objective about our instincts. As such, Mercury's position in a horoscope reveals a person's general ability to communicate ideas through the written or spoken word. In this respect, Mercury is the ruler of that very actively communicative and mental sign, Gemini. Mercury is also the ruler of Virgo. Virgo is an earthy sign and quite practical by nature. When Mercury is in this sign in a person's chart, all mental activity is usually geared to material and pragmatic ends. To find out where Mercury or any of the other planets are in your chart, you will need to consult an ephemeris (see "An Astrological Glossary,").

Mercury's Associations

Sign rulership: Gemini and Virgo

Gemstones: Agate, marble, topaz, aquamarine

Metal: Quicksilver

Day of the week: Wednesday

Colors: Pale blue, silver

Plants, herbs, and flowers: Azalea, calamint, caraway, carrot, dill, endive, fennel, hazel, lavender, licorice, lily of the valley, mulberry, parsley, valerian, wild carrot

Parts of the body: Nervous system, thyroid gland, vocal cords, hands

Psychological principle: Rational thought

Psychological dynamics and keywords:
  positive—rational, clever, intelligent, communicative, informative
  negative—overly intellectual, restless, chatty, indiscriminate, dualistic, manipulative

Psychological attributes: Intellect, logic, reason, speech, language, learning

Areas of interest: Accounting, engineering, writing, teaching journalism, media, speaking, book selling, clerks, agents of all kinds

Spiritual principles: Messenger of the Gods, Divine Communicator

VENUS

Many people prefer Venus to all the other heavenly bodies, for she is the goddess of love and money. Venus is that force within each person that indicates one's ability to attract others. She is the power of personal magnetism that can be used (or abused!) in terms of our intimate or financial relationships.

As the ruler of Libra, the sign of marriage and partnerships, Venus is very much involved with making people and their surroundings beautiful. Let a Libra into your house and he or she will definitely decorate it, either by actually moving things around or just by being there! Venus always attempts to "soften the edges" so that life's experiences are made that much more pleasant. She is the part of our nature that corresponds to the artist, the poet, and most of all, the romantic. Her placement in your horoscope tells you a lot about your aesthetic tastes, creative skills, and your ability to attract Venus' material and emotional blessings. Most of all, Venus speaks to you about your relationships and as such is of paramount importance to your love life.

In her rulership over her second sign, Taurus, Venus is more concerned with physical appearances and the material considerations of life. Thus she is involved with banking, real estate, commodities, and investments. Venus when ruling Taurus has as her goals comfort, abundance, and beauty. These blessings are not just for herself, however; we have to remember that she is also the ruler of Libra and thus is always involved in bringing her bounty into the lives of her partners and loved ones as well.

Venus' Associations

Sign rulership: Libra and Taurus

Gemstones: Carnelian, coral, jade, alabaster, beryl

Metals: Copper, brass

Day of the week: Friday

Colors: Yellow, pale blue, green, pastels

Plants, herbs, and flowers: Clover, daffodil, ferns, goldenrod, gooseberry, lily, mint, pennyroyal, peppermint, rose, spearmint, wheat, violet

Parts of the body: Kidneys, urinary tract

Psychological principle: Personal magnetism

Psychological dynamics and keywords:

    positive—socially poised, graceful, affectionate, poetic, artistic, harmonious, pleasure-seeking and pleasure-giving

    negative—lazy, superficial, gaudy, vulgar, excessively lustful

Psychological attributes: Cohesion, aesthetics, refinement, elegance, balance, symmetry, melody, rhythm

Areas of interest: Music, painting, song, dance, poetry, acting, clothing and interior design, relationships

Spiritual principles: Personal love, beauty

MARS

Mars is both the partner and the opposite of Venus. While Venus brings us union, Mars urges separation. When Venus sings to us of love and recites poetry, Mars pursues us with sexual needs and desires and tells of victories on the battle-field. Mars bestows upon the individual the ability to stand forth and assert himself. He represents the strength of the ego in action, giving us the courage and confidence to move ahead with life. When Mars is too strong, he brings out the baser emotional drives of life in crude and rude ways. When Mars is a balanced influence in a horoscope, he gives one the ability to say, "I am myself and no one else, and that self is good." Also called the "Red Planet," Mars' color lets us know that he is a planetary power of force and action.

Most people require a relatively strong, though not overpowering, Mars in their charts—otherwise we have lit-tle in the way of self-assertion. Mars gives the courage and stamina to endure the pressures of life. Mars is the urge to win and succeed; at the very least, he helps us to survive! Mars confers the ability to strive for what we desire, and if well placed in our birth map, he gives the ability to cut through the "red tape" of life and go right to the heart of each and every issue facing us.

The above characteristics are associated with Mars' two signs: Aries and Scorpio. Both of these signs prefer to be quite direct, but there is a difference. Aries is the open-faced warrior who stands right up to you, projecting his fiery martial energy overtly for all to see. Scorpio is more of the spy, working behind the scenes. Scorpio is direct in that he never loses sight of his objective and works away at it until his watery martial energy breaks down all resistance.

In his higher way of functioning, Mars is the champion of justice and the defender of the weak and downtrodden. In his lower aspect, Mars represents what is still the unredeemed animal in humankind. Mars is then seen as the baser emotional drives and the blind, instinctive aggression unfortunately still so prevalent among many of us. Mars can be either the avenger or the redeemer, but in whichever capacity, he is a strong and mighty force.

Mars' Associations

Sign rulership: Aries and Scorpio
Gemstones: Jasper, bloodstone, flint, malachite
Metals: Iron, steel
Day of the week: Tuesday
Colors: Scarlet, carmine, magenta, deep orange
Plants, herbs, and flowers: Onion, garlic, hops, horseradish, mustard, ginger, hemlock, cactus, gentian, basil, capers, mousetail, savin, wormwood
Parts of the body: the head in general, especially the nose, chin, and right eye; muscle tissues; red blood cells
Psychological principle: Personal drive, projection of ego
Psychological dynamics and keywords:
   positive—courage, independence, initiative, drive, passion
   negative—aggressive, violent, impulsive, egocentric, wantonly destructive, cruel, sexually irresponsible
Psychological attributes: Assertive, direct, forceful, competitive, sexual, energy of the ego, urge to win
Areas of interest: Military, surgery, athletics, engineering, use of sharp objects
Spiritual principles: Regeneration, redemption

JUPITER

4

Jupiter is a planet of good fortune. He brings abundance into your life, both on material and spiritual levels. He is the force that gives us the urge to explore life through philosophy, religion, and long-distance travel. Jupiter is also the jovial entrepreneur and businessman who is very happy when you have more money than you need, rich food, and beautiful homes and cars. Jupiter likes people to smile and enjoy life. Yet when Jupiter's influence is too strong in a chart, a person may become a religious fanatic or so greedy for money and the "good life" that he is never satisfied with the blessings right in front of him.

Jupiter acts not only to expand your material well-being (and often your waistline as well!), he is very much involved in the development of your higher mental attributes. In this respect, Jupiter as the ruler of the philosopher's sign, Sagittarius, is connected with higher education and the urge to evolve a wider vision of life. Jupiter takes us beyond the rational mind of Mercury. Mercury is basically concerned with communicating ideas, but Jupiter is involved with the creation of ideals and principles. Jupiter gives the gift of prophecy, while Mercury chooses the words through which these divine revelations are expressed.

Jupiter's other sign is Pisces, and the Fish swims in a boundless ocean. Jupiter is not one to be contained or restrained. He is the ruler of long-distance travel, and his ticket has no restrictions placed upon it. This can work for or against people, depending on their level of psychological maturity. Excesses of love, charity, and knowledge are gifts that can be bestowed and shared. But Jupiter can also give gluttony, waste, and unbridled self-indulgence. In this respect, it is good to have a harmonious relationship to Saturn in the chart, as this influence, as we shall see next, does a great deal to modify Jupiter's more flagrant behavior.

Jupiter's Associations

Sign rulership: Sagittarius and Pisces
Gemstones: Amethyst, hyacinth, topaz
Metal: Tin
Day of the week: Thursday
Colors: Blue, violet, purple, indigo
Plants, herbs, and flowers: Asparagus, chestnut, clove, currant, daisy, dandelion, leek, mint, nutmeg, strawberry, sugar cane
Parts of the body: Posterior pituitary gland, thighs, hips, liver
Psychological principle: Expansion
Psychological dynamics and keywords:
    positive—philosophical insight, optimism, expanded
            vision, enthusiasm, generosity, kindness
    negative—excessiveness, exaggeration, fanaticism, self-
            indulgence
Psychological attributes: Attitude of abundance and prosperity, benevolence, aspiration, morals, ethics, faith, hope, trust
Areas of interest: Politics, law, philosophy, ministry, religion, philanthropy
Spiritual principles: Aspiration to the life of the Soul

SATURN

♄

Saturn's influence is very much the opposite but is also the complement to Jupiter's. While Jupiter expands, Saturn contracts. When Jupiter is at play, Saturn is hard at work. As Jupiter looks for ways to gamble and speculate, Saturn finds ways for solid, risk-free investments. Just as Jupiter represents the kindly, overly indulgent uncle, Saturn is more often than not the stern, authoritarian father, demanding that you learn self-discipline in order to grow and prosper. Saturn is the Law, and he requires a person to learn correct behavior in life. Self-mastery is Saturn's goal.

Saturn may act as the Teacher in your life, a wise older friend who tells you: "Listen, young one, to the voice of ancient truth and proven experience. Before you continue to the next stage in your life, you must grasp the real meaning of all that you have done that has brought you to this place. In order for you to expand your material worth, social position, or knowledge, you must first learn responsibility, structure, order, and form. Once you have correctly mastered these laws and principles of life, you will have the foundation you need for success." In this respect, Saturn is the ruler of the sign Capricorn. It is through Capricorn that we achieve our social and spiritual goals. As you will see in the next chapter, Capricorn has its definite struggles and challenges, but its reward is anchored achievement and solid growth. Saturn is also closely connected to Aquarius. It is the job of the Water Bearer to build social structures and networks of interpersonal contacts so that there is ease of communication in the world.

In the physical body, Saturn rules the backbone, for without an erect spine, the entire body will collapse. If that occurs, it would be impossible for us to enjoy Uncle Jupiter's elaborate vacations—or anything else, for that matter! A strong and positive Saturn in your horoscope gives determination for success and the ability to structure and prioritize thoughts and actions. A difficult Saturn in the chart brings a deep sense of limitation and self-doubt.

Saturn's Associations

Sign rulership: Capricorn and Aquarius

Gemstones: Sapphire, lapis lazuli, jet

Metal: Lead

Day of the week: Saturday

Colors: Grey, black, dark brown, deep green

Plants, herbs, and flowers: Barley, parsnip, spinach, nightshade, moss, holly, wintergreen, mandrake, senna, tamarisk, ivy, vervain, rue, comfrey, hemlock

Parts of the body: Medullary portion of the adrenal gland, skin, teeth, bones, joints, gall bladder, spine

Psychological principle: Order

Psychological dynamics and keywords:
    positive—organizational ability, systematic, analytical, responsible, patient
    negative—manipulative, pessimistic, repressed, fearful, inhibiting, fatalistic

Psychological attributes: Form, structure, shape, wisdom, organization, concentration, prudence

Areas of interest: Business, real estate, banking, construction, investing, politics, administration, mining, undertaking

Spiritual principles: Karma (Law of Cause and Effect)

Uranus, Neptune, and Pluto represent forces and energies that work to establish us more on spiritual levels. Saturn is the most distant planet a person can see with the naked eye. It represents the limits of what we could call the normal, everyday life of our personalities. Once we move on to the three outermost planets, we "move up an octave" in life, so to speak, and the cosmos plays us a different tune.

URANUS

Uranus is the eccentric of the solar system—the only planet that revolves on its equator, pointing its north pole to the Sun! It is Uranus that helps us to unfold our individuality and the expression of that creative spark within us which, when developed, gives us a deeper connection to life.

Uranus is said to be the "higher octave" of Mercury. While Mercury governs reason and the rational mind, Uranus is connected to the power of intuition. It is Uranus that ignites that special spark of mental lightning that illuminates our understanding of complex problems and issues in a flash. It is Uranus that allows us to penetrate into the heart of any situation without having to take the slower route of reasoning and rationalization. We know simply because we know. When Uranus is too strong in a horoscope, he makes for a person who is very erratic and willful, undependable and unreliable. When positive in the chart, he makes for a highly gifted, original, and inventive individual in any number of fields of endeavor.

Uranus is the primary ruler of Aquarius (with Saturn's influence a strong secondary factor). Aquarians and other people highly affected by the influence of this erratic planet will find that they are extremely independent, self-willed, and certainly reluctant to be controlled by any externally imposed rules and regulations. The true "Uranian" is very idealistic and always working to achieve some envisioned social goal. Uranus is future-oriented, and those individuals under his rays are rebels and revolutionaries, constantly at work to break down traditional patterns and structures.

Uranus' Associations

Sign rulership: Aquarius

Gemstones: Amber, ruby, carnelian, hyacinth

Metal: Uranium

Day of the week: none

Colors: Light azure, silvery-white

Plants, herbs, and flowers: None that are traditionally associated with this planet. We could say, however, that hybrid variations of plants can be connected to Uranus, as this is the planet of all types of inventions, organic or inorganic.

Parts of the body: Parathyroid gland, brain and nervous system, pituitary gland

Psychological principle: Intuition

Psychological dynamics and keywords:
    positive—innovative, humane, progressive, inventive,
    negative—willfully destructive, anarchistic, fanatical,
            unpredictable, irresponsible

Psychological attributes: Rebellious, original, altruistic, platonic, independent, reformative, freedom-loving, genius, nonconformist

Areas of interest: Inventing, science, theory, media, electronics, astrology, psychology, metaphysics, aviation, civic organizations, computers

Spiritual principle: Individualization

NEPTUNE

Neptune is the "higher octave" of Venus. While Venus exalts the beauty of personal love and right human relationships, Neptune is the planet that brings us the understanding of spiritual love: sacrificial, transpersonal, and transformative. These qualities are also found in the special sharing that some personal love relationships bring into our lives. When this happens, you can be sure that this is the force of Neptune working through his daughter, Venus. In essence, Venus brings in the love of the personality while Neptune reveals the love of the Soul. Yet Neptune has another, more obscure side to his nature. When he is too strong or not well placed in the horoscope, he is apt to bring confusion and lack of discrimination in love. He can encourage escapism through drugs and other forms of addiction. Yet Neptune is also the ruler of healers, those men and woman using natural and chemical substances to aid humanity. All such medicines are also under the direct influence of Neptune.

Neptune is the ruler of Pisces, a sign of the watery element and therefore intimately connected to different emotional currents. Neptune speaks through the emotional nature, bringing either disillusion or illumination (and everything else in between!). Neptune is the heavenly musician, the force that makes people swoon with the beauty of a symphony or the high notes of an aria. Neptune is the grand patron of the ballet, the inspiring force of dancers. It is Neptune who allows the dancer to merge with the music, extending its rhythms out to you through her physical movements. Neptune is the artist's muse, while Venus gives the artist the various forms for his creative expression. Finally, Neptune is the mystic and the clairvoyant—individuals whose sensitivity is so subtle that ordinary boundaries of perception melt away into the waters of inspiration. But beware! Neptune is also the fakir and spiritual charlatan.

Neptune's Associations

Sign rulership: Pisces
Gemstones: Emerald, agate, marble, selenite, aquamarine, amethyst
Metals: Platinum, lithium
Day of the week: none
Colors: White, mauve, lavender, black, sea-green
Plants, herbs, and flowers: Poppies, hallucinogenic mush-rooms
Part of the body: Pineal gland
Psychological principles: Self-sacrifice, empathy
Psychological dynamics and keywords:
    positive—compassionate, inclusive, loving, mystical
    negative—escapist, deluded, emotionally chaotic, unreal-
        istic, deceitful
Psychological attributes: Universal in orientation, visionary, lacking boundaries, emotionally motivated and directed
Areas of interest: Art, writing, acting, photography, film-making, asceticism, mysticism, philosophy, occultism, socialized medicine, charities
Spiritual principle: Love—impersonal, transpersonal, and unconditional

PLUTO

P

Pluto is the planet farthest away from the Sun and in many ways the most mysterious of the heavenly bodies in its effects on us. This dark world represents the deep inner powers of renewal and regeneration. Pluto is death, but he is also the vehicle for new life. As the "higher octave" of Mars, Pluto's effects go beyond warfare and sexual desire. If nations go to war under the influence of Mars, Pluto indicates the new societies that rise from the rubble. If, through the stimulating influence of the Red Planet, two people are sexually attracted to each other, it is Pluto that ushers in a new generation through conception and birth. When Pluto is positively placed in a horoscope, it indicates the use of your personal willpower to bring about healthy changes your life. When too strong an influence, Pluto indicates a destructive person who may be overly manipulative in dealing with others.

Pluto is the planetary ruler of Scorpio and also closely associated with Aries. In Scorpio we find the principle of death but also the promise of renewal and regeneration. This principle is strongly at work in Aries, which is the first sign of spring and the potential of new life. Pluto's effects may seem to express themselves through sudden explosiveness, but the underground potency of Pluto's power has been gaining momentum for a long time.

Pluto's Associations

Sign rulership: Scorpio and Aries

Gemstones: Beryl, jade

Metals: Tungsten, plutonium

Day of the week: none

Colors: Dark red, black

Plants, herbs, and flowers: None that are traditionally associated with this planet.

Parts of the body: Pancreas, colon, reproductive system

Psychological principle: Transformation

Psychological dynamics and keywords:
    positive—regenerative, renewing, transformational,
              healing
    negative—manipulative, seductive, power-hungry, willful

Psychological attributes: Death, rebirth, annihilation, release, cleansing, creation, sex, resurrection, metamorphosis, transmutation, revitalization, hidden power

Areas of interest: Psychoanalysis, healing, surgery, demolition, politics, atomic energy

Spiritual principles: Transcending the ego, redemption

The Twelve Signs
of the Zodiac

Each of us is a composite picture of all the signs of the zodiac. We are a Taurus when we go to the bank, a Gemini when we travel to work or school, a Sagittarius when we visit our place of worship, a Capricorn when we make an investment, a Pisces when we wander about in our dreams and aspirations, a Scorpio when we make love, an Aries when we seek a new direction for our lives, a Leo when we are creative, a Virgo when we improve upon what has been created, a Libra when we are in relationship with another, a Cancer when we are at home, and an Aquarius when we work with others to help people. The particular sign that matters most to you—and the astrological indication easiest to determine—is your Sun Sign. This we can discover just by knowing the date of your birth.

Please note: The signs of the zodiac, just like the people of the Earth, are gender-equal—half are male and half are female. The male signs are Aries, Gemini, Leo, Libra, Sagittarius, and Aquarius. The female signs are Taurus, Cancer, Virgo, Scorpio, Capricorn, and Pisces. This male-and femaleness has little to do with human masculinity or femininity. It merely means that the male signs are "electric" and projective in nature while the female signs are "magnetic" and receptive. Marilyn Monroe, a Gemini, projected an incredible amount of femininity, while Martin Luther King, Jr., a Capricorn, held an amazing degree of magnetic strength and power. To make the writing about the zodiac gender-equal as well, we will use the words "he" and "him" when speaking about the six so-called male signs, and "she" and "her" when discussing the six female ones.

Important: You may find that the last day of one astrological sign overlaps the first day of the following sign. This is due to the fact that there are slight fluctuations in the movements of the heavens, leading to some yearly differences in the boundaries of the signs. If your birthdate falls on the first or last day of a sign, you are said to be "cuspal" in nature, meaning that you will have characteristics of both signs. It is possible to know with great accuracy your actual Sun Sign, but this can only be determined by an astrologer making the necessary mathematical calculations. Many metaphysical bookstores can offer you this service or let you know where such information may be obtained.

ARIES—THE RAM
MARCH 20–APRIL 20

 I Am, Therefore I Am

All of life is energy, and Aries seems to have a natural abundance of it. This is only natural, as Aries is the first sign of the zodiac, the initiator of life's creative potential. Aries begins on the first day of spring of each year. Spring is the season that brings people, animals, and plants out of the quietude of winter and into the explosive process of new birth.

The child of the Ram is much like a toddler who has just learned how to walk. He is aggressively aware of himself (to the exclusion of potential surrounding dangers) and demands constant attention. Although warm and affectionate by nature, he is also always on guard. Aries is quick to respond to mistreatment of any kind, either to himself or to others. Most of all, he is filled with strength, potential, and passion of life.

With the courage of his ruling planet, Mars (the god of war), Aries is always either preparing for or setting forth into the world in search of new horizons to conquer. But he must also find the necessary practical foundation for his adventures. His inner questions are: "How may I best mobilize all the energy within myself so that the greatest response may come from life? How may I establish myself as a separate and complete individual among so many other individuals in the world?"

Aries is very good at inspiring others, motivating the life around him in ways that push his plans and projects forward. Aries is definitely the leader, even if he is only leading himself! Aries is very direct in his approach to life. In fact, many people find him too confrontational, as he wastes little time with diplomacy or subtlety. It is his straightforwardness and sense of direction that are his special tools for his own and everyone else's benefit. The strong and mature Aries never accepts obstacles as finalities. He will use his abundant creative will to go forward and try again until victory is achieved.

Aries' greatest blind spot, one that may often impede his success in life, is the tendency for him to be aware only of himself, his particular needs, and his desires. He may have a difficult time dealing harmoniously with others—"compromise" is a very "non-Aries" word! This gives him the reputation of being pushy and egocentric. The force of Aries' fiery nature is such that he is often unaware of the more delicate aspects of many social situations. He may be so concerned with expressing his own opinions all of the time that he easily overrides others in his attempt to take command.

We should remember that not all Aries are rams; some are lambs. Many of these spring children are quite unsure of themselves. Yet unlike their animal counterparts, these human lambs are not easily shepherded. Even the most timid of Aries individuals has a distinct need to find his own path in life, even if he is not sure exactly where he is going. He knows that someway, somehow, sometime, his road will become clear to him and he will be walking upon it.

When Aries feels self-confident, there is no one more energetic. Aries is the sign of raw and unchanneled energy. He is a person of little patience, meeting the challenges of life head-on. There can be few sidetracks on the road he travels, although he does find himself on dead-end streets once in a while. In this case he merely bangs his head through the brick wall and creates another avenue upon which to continue his journey.

Aries is a passionate sign and feels very strongly about the people he loves. He is highly prioritized in his affection and usually more prone to monogamy than to promiscuity. Yet he is also easily bored and restless by nature, and if he is emotionally immature, that monogamy can be of the serial kind, one in which Aries moves from one partner to another in quick succession. Yet if Aries finds that his relationship allows him the personal freedom which he requires in order to be himself, he is a very devoted partner. People in relationship with Aries will find his enthusiasm for life, his initiative, his courage, and his highly charged romanticism very appealing. They may even forgive his headstrong shortsightedness!

The Aries List

Ruling planets: Mars and Pluto

Gemstones: Diamond, bloodstone

Metals: Tungsten, iron

Plants, herbs, and flowers: Holly, thistle, nettles, onions, fern, mustard

Day of the week: Tuesday

Number: 1

Color: Scarlet

Element: Fire

Quality: Cardinal (See "An Astrological Glossary" for a description of the qualities.)

Parts of the body: Head, especially the eyes; brain

Psychological characteristics and keywords: Courageous, bold, energetic, fervent, initiatory, direct, decisive, spontaneous, competitive, foolhardy, impatient, hot-headed, uncontrollable, self-centered, impulsive, opinionated

Professions: Explorer, leader, soldier, engineer, policeman, adventurer, fireman, athlete

Primary principle: Activity

Biggest virtue: Initiative

Biggest flaw: Impulsiveness

Best signs for relationships: Leo, Sagittarius, Aquarius, Gemini

Spiritual impulse: The will to initiate creativity

Famous Aries individuals: Harry Houdini, Vincent van Gogh, Hugh Hefner, Charlie Chaplin, Joan Crawford, Bette Davis, Warren Beatty, Leonardo da Vinci, Marlon Brando, Diana Ross

TAURUS—THE BULL
APRIL 21–MAY 20

 I Have, Therefore I Am

Although spring begins in Aries, by the time the Sun has moved into Taurus, the creative powers of life are in full force. It is during this part of the year that the abundance and natural splendor of the Earth are everywhere to behold. All the trees and plants are in bloom, and both the animal and the human kingdoms are involved in those vigorous rites of courtship that culminate in Gemini's June weddings.

The Taurean individual is full of the creative passion of spring and is by nature the most sensual, and certainly one of the most romantic, of all the signs. After all, her ruling planet is the goddess of love (and money!), Venus. Taurus is, in fact, a very fertile sign. Her intense magnetism is such that she is easily capable of bringing all the necessary material and human support in her life that she may ever need. Astrologers say that "a child of Venus never wants," and although many Taureans are often too concerned about love and money, they have a definite astrological advantage in both of these important areas of life.

What you say about yourself and your life, you will create. It is worrying about lacks in either love or money that can bring real problems into a Taurus' life. Taurus is the ruling sign of the throat and the vocal cords. When the power of the word is added to their natural strength and intense determination, Taureans, more than any other sign, can create their own destiny. If Taureans have learned the difference between love and lust, need and greed, having and sharing, then all of life's springtime bounty is theirs to enjoy, and their destiny will be a beautiful one.

Taurus is Mother Earth. Her feelings, like the richness within the Earth itself, lie buried deep within her. On the surface Taurus may appear to be tranquil and unmoving, but then, very suddenly, the Earth begins to tremble and a great quake takes place. For this reason, the usual placidity and supportive Taurean nature should not be taken for granted. Taurus is loyal and steadfast, true and steady, but do not betray her, do not deceive her. Her temper is slow to erupt, but when it does, the earth will move from under the feet of the unlucky person who is the butt of the Bull's anger.

The blessings of Venus also give Taurus a strong love of the arts and everything that is beautiful. When that blessing is extended, Taurus may find herself very gifted in these areas. Yet as a "fixed" (and rather stubborn) sign, Taurus

often finds that she needs some outside push to get on with her life. If she is pushed too hard, however, this same fixity of nature will turn into incredible resistance. It is then that Taurean determination becomes Taurean repression and nothing gets done, ever!

Taurus may suffer from extreme inertia. By nature, she does not like change, especially those changes brought about by others and thus not under her control. Taurus can be very cautious, and this can lead either to an astute sense of timing or a complete paralysis of action. Taurus prefers to engage in projects that have already proven their worth. She is usually not very good at initiating what is new and original but is very gifted at sustaining and enriching those efforts started by others. Taurus must believe in the true value and inner worth of something or someone, however, before she gives such support.

In relationships, Taurus tends to be monogamous, preferring to anchor and solidify her love and loyalty within the bonds of deep commitment. Taurus wants to build upon what she sees in her beloved. She has the ability to see deeply into another's real worth, and she holds firmly to her faith in that vision. Taurus is easily pleased by good food, fine fabrics, and soft (but consistent) caresses. She is also very practical.

Her fundamental understanding of life and her keen common sense are among her best natural attributes. Of all the signs, Taurus is the one most closely connected to the Earth and the physical body.

The Taurus List

Ruling planet: Venus

Gemstones: Emerald, jade, coral

Metals: Copper, brass

Plants, herbs, and flowers: Moss, lilies, daisies, dandelion, larkspur, flax, myrtle

Day of the week: Friday

Number: 2

Colors: Green, mustard yellow

Element: Earth

Quality: Fixed

Parts of the body: Neck, throat, and ears; thyroid gland

Psychological characteristics and keywords: Loyal, deliberate, cautious, grounded, generous, sensuous, practical, affectionate, productive, stubborn, hedonistic, unreasonable, unbending, immovable, possessive, materialistic

Professions: Agriculturalist, artist, sculptor, actor, dancer, designer of clothes, singer, real-estate agent

Primary principle: Bringing shape and form to ideas

Biggest virtue: Productivity

Biggest flaw: Stubbornness

Best signs for relationships: Capricorn, Virgo, Pisces, Sagittarius

Spiritual impulse: The will to materialize the forms of life

Famous Taurus individuals: Shirley MacLaine, Queen Elizabeth, Barbra Streisand, Salvador Dali, Bono, William Shakespeare, Karl Marx, Socrates, Sigmund Freud, Katharine Hepburn

GEMINI—THE TWINS
MAY 21–JUNE 20

♊ *I Think, Therefore I Am*

Gemini is an airy, communicative sign, ruled by the fleet-footed Mercury—in Greek mythology, the messenger of the gods. Gemini is constantly on the move. His mind is always alive with ideas and the need to relate, talk, and connect. Gemini is constantly analyzing life, separating thoughts into smaller individual pieces. Although this tendency can and does often make for a highly intelligent, versatile, and gifted mind, Gemini may find himself equally spun out, dispersed, and nervous.

The symbol for Gemini is the roman numeral II. This glyph reveals Gemini's basic dualistic nature. Gemini must relate, and relating takes more than one person or idea. Therefore, to Gemini's way of thinking and acting, the more he can do, the more places he can go, and the more information he knows, the larger is his sense of personal identity. Gemini's sense of self is always saying, "Multiply me, multiply me!" and Gemini tries to do just that through his incredibly busy life and consistently busy mind.

Gemini is often called the "Child of the Zodiac" because of his youthful vitality, his avid curiosity, and his tremendous need to ask the question "Why?" As not every question can be answered (or even has an answer), we often find the most unsatisfied Geminis among the most intelligent. Gemini finds it very difficult to unite his two basic sides: the intellectual and the emotional. Once these two parts of himself are unified, wisdom will flourish, the mind will ripen, and many of his questions will answer themselves.

As the child develops the necessary skills to go out into the world, his scope of experiences widens and he creates the foundation upon which he can base the rest of his life. Gemini is always going into life to collect such experiences, but often the foundation eludes him. He gets lost in the excitement of the experiences themselves. As a person matures, he begins to pick and choose what is correct for himself. A mature Gemini can also arrive at this point; he just delays this effort at discrimination as long as possible. Gemini likes variety and the ability to be in as many places as possible almost at the same time. He loves the many faces he meets, the numerous adventures which call to him, and the versatility of his own mercurial nature.

A Gemini is a fascinating partner to have in relationships, provided you have the strength and interest to keep up with him. He prefers short stories to novels, plays in four acts rather than one, MTV to a concert, a buffet rather than a sit-down dinner, and music that has many quick-changing tempos rather than a slow, consistent beat. In terms of travel, Gemini definitely prefers to visit seven cities in Italy in seven days, for example, rather than spend the whole week in Rome. If he has two televisions, he has no problem watching them both simultaneously, and two cars (both for him!) are definitely better than one.

Yes, you need plenty of pep to play with Gemini. You also have to be free of jealousy. Gemini is very flirtatious and enjoys speaking and joking with everyone. He is very charming. This charm does not necessarily mean that he will be romantically linked to that beautiful person he was speaking with at the party instead of you. Nevertheless, he will definitely enjoy himself. He is quick with words that are not always followed by actions. He may repeat himself and then forget what he has just said or promised. Yet when he wants to do so, he can write six wonderful letters in less than an hour and return all of those outstanding phone calls, saving you the trouble of having to do so.

Gemini is fun, no doubt about it. And when the "Child of the Zodiac" finally becomes an adult, we may just find an incredibly gifted person. This is a Gemini with both clear and intelligent powers of reasoning and a sense of playfulness that brings a great deal of joy into any surroundings. We then see that the child is not lost but is alive and well, safely inside Gemini's heart.

The Gemini List

Ruling planet: Mercury
Gemstones: Topaz, agate
Metal: Quicksilver
Plants, herbs, and flowers: Yarrow, woodbine, vervain, tansy, doggrass, madder
Day of the week: Wednesday
Number: 5
Color: Crystal blue
Element: Air
Quality: Mutable
Parts of the body: Hands and arms; lungs; thymus gland
Psychological characteristics and keywords: Lighthearted, cheerful, clever, witty, intelligent, adaptable, communicative, alert, overintellectual, wordy, unfocused, nervous, excitable, fickle, unemotional, indiscriminate
Professions: Secretary, writer, teacher, journalist, messenger, lecturer, printer, book-seller, linguist, broadcaster
Primary principle: The rational mind
Biggest virtue: Intelligence
Biggest flaw: Superficiality
Best signs for relationships: Aquarius, Libra, Aries, Leo
Spiritual impulse: The will to communicate
Famous Gemini individuals: John F. Kennedy, Marilyn Monroe, Bob Hope, Bob Dylan, Paul McCartney, Queen Victoria, John Wayne, Henry Kissinger, Judy Garland, Anne Frank

CANCER—THE CRAB
JUNE 21–JULY 22

 I Feel, Therefore I Am

If you were to choose one word to best describe Cancer, that word would be "feelings." Cancer is the sign most closely associated with home and mother. In this respect, almost all Cancers have an incredibly strong relationship to their infancy and childhood. If those stages of their lives were healthy, strong, and supportive, Cancer is a very positive, emotionally nurturing individual. Her compassion may then be used for the well-being of all other people in her environment. This is the kind of Cancer who always says, "Come over to my house for dinner. There's plenty of food and comfort available."

But should a Cancer have a difficult childhood, one with an absent or non-nurturing mother, then we have a very wounded Crab indeed. In this case, we find a Cancer who is constantly searching for emotional security and almost never finding it. It is not that life is not capable of bringing her such safety. It is just that if Cancer cannot build a secure foundation inside herself, she will not be able to recognize it outside herself.

The wounded Cancer is a person who expects others to be constantly supportive of her needs and weaknesses. In this case, the deep feelings of the Crab are totally turned inward and her need is for everyone else to nurture her. We then have a Cancer always asking, "Can I come over to your house for dinner? Is there plenty of food and comfort available for me?" But once Cancer's healing is accomplished, once her emotional foundation is firm, then we have a wonderful supplier of emotional strength and support.

Cancer is very connected to the past and is always collecting both objects and memories. She is nostalgic and sentimental, and her inner and outer storehouses are full. Cancer never forgets, especially when her memory is connected to one of the five senses. Not only will she always recall a face, she will also remember the smell of her grandmother's perfume, the feel of a loving hand, the taste of her sixteenth birthday cake, and the sound of her father snoring.

In relationships, Cancer usually acts in one of two ways. The immature Cancer is always the insecure baby, ever in need of some form of nurturing. This kind of Cancer will often attract people to her who need to be needed. The more mature Crab has an inner sense of give and take. She instinctively knows when there is a real emotional need that should be supported or sustained. These Cancers have tremendous inner resourcefulness and a most delightful and surprising way to offer what is theirs to give.

If you are looking for an intimate kind of person in a relationship, then look no further than the nearest beach and you will find your Crab. Cancers certainly love the water, but water in the astrological sense means emotions. You have to be ready to experience closely the depth of human feelings when you are connected to a Cancer. If you are the more mental, detached kind of person, then Cancer is definitely not your sign. And if you are a Cancer, take care that you are aware of and respect your own sensitivity when choosing a partner.

Cancer is a sign that seeks to protect the person she loves. Almost all Cancers of either sex are very maternal by nature. Perhaps the only exception to this is found among Cancers who deny their feelings and live in pain. These individuals have to learn how to come out of themselves so that they may feed others with love. Speaking of feeding, almost all Cancers are at home either in the kitchen or in restaurants. Like their Taurean sisters, Cancers believe in the healing nature of food and love to eat—and feed others as well!

When the warm waters of the Crab are full of nutriments, the children in her world are safe, secure, protected, and abundant. Cancer will entertain, enchant, care for, and nurture all who come into her magical realm. She is a daughter of the Moon, after all, and her sense of the mystical and the incredible is a most profound part of her nature.

The Cancer List

Ruling planet: Moon

Gemstones: Pearl, moonstone

Metals: Silver, aluminum

Plants, herbs, and flowers: Cucumbers, squash, melons, and all plants that grow in water, such as water lilies and rushes

Day of the week: Monday

Number: 3

Color: Silvery-blue

Element: Water

Quality: Cardinal

Parts of the body: Chest and breasts, stomach, pancreas, liver, womb

Psychological characteristics and keywords: Emotional, sensitive, nurturing, empathic, protective, intuitive, sustaining, moody, oversensitive, clinging, paranoid, overbearing, needy, overemotional, dependent

Professions: Homemaker, nurse, fisherman, sailor, social worker, home-care provider, clairvoyant, prophet, medium, pre-school teacher, interior designer, architect, cook

Primary principle: Nourishment

Biggest virtue: Care

Biggest flaw: Insecurity

Best signs for relationships: Scorpio, Pisces, Taurus, Virgo

Spiritual impulse: Compassion

Famous Cancer individuals: Rembrandt, Princess Diana, Ringo Starr, Nelson Rockefeller, Robin Williams, Bill Cosby, Abigail van Buren ("Dear Abby") and Ann Landers (sisters), Lena Horne, Linda Ronstadt, Dianne Feinstein (U.S Senator from California)

LEO—THE LION
JULY 23–AUGUST 23

♌ *I Will, Therefore I Am*

We can understand so much about Leo when we know that the part of the body ruled by the Lion is the heart. The heart is the center of the circulatory system, and it is also the center of life. In the same way, Leo is the center of every life situation in which he finds himself. To the immature Lion, this gives rise to a very egocentric nature, one in which Leo will demand all the attention from any group or social circumstance. His sense of self-importance can be somewhat exaggerated, and he may easily have his feelings hurt when he is not given the attention he believes is "the right of kings."

The mature Leo is quite different. His light comes from a very strong and anchored center, and it is from this point that Leo gives and gives and then gives some more. He is truly a child of the Sun, and the Sun never exhausts its fuel. This is the kind of Leo who radiates power, joy, goodwill, and abundance for all to share. He is loyal and generous to his friends, passionate to his lovers, and creative in all he says and does. He loves children, especially his own, and they love him in return.

The heart is that part of ourselves in which many of our highest virtues are thought to reside: honor, faithfulness, truth, and trust. Many Leos embody these fine qualities and have a way of bringing them out in others. The Lion is a noble beast inspiring courage, kindness, confidence, and consistency of character. Leo is usually physically strong by nature. He rarely falls ill and if he does, he recuperates quickly. Yet his greatest strength is also his weakness—his heart.

Leo can be rather naive in relationships. His passion is often so strong, his affections so deep, his ardor so intense, that he may fail to see the reality of the other person's feelings. Leo has to be careful not to be one person loving for two. He should be aware of the nature of his loved one's affections, changes of moods, and subtle emotions. Leo may be brave, generous, and potent but he is definitely not subtle! He can go through life believing that others will love him at the same level of intensity that he is feeling for them when this may not be the case at all.

Leo also has to watch out for flattery. He tends to be rather gullible and open to believing what he wishes to believe. Image is usually very important to the Lion, who loves clothing, jewelry, and all of life's finery. He can be stopped in his fiery tracks by a flirtatious look or a complimentary word. Leo is not a schemer. It's hard for him to hide anything. He is very out-front about his life, and his expressive face tells the whole story of how he is feeling at any given moment.

One of the most important characteristics about Leo is his intense creative drive. The theater and the arts in general all come under his rulership, and Leo's sense of the dramatic is well known among astrologers. Leo loves to dramatize himself. He is the writer, director, producer, and especially the star of his own movie. What is important for him to remember is that he should take some time out to watch his movie and not just be in it.

One of the difficulties people find with Leo is his tendency to be self-centered. Leo is ruled by the Sun, and the Sun is the heart of the solar system. All the planets get their light from the Sun, and they all revolve around this central star. Leo can act in much the same way, playing favorites and carefully choosing which one of his "planets" receives any light. Leo can often mistake his friends for "admirers" and set himself above and apart from them. Needless to say, this does not result in equality of relationship, and then Leo wonders why he is rebuked and left out of certain social situations.

The real king of the zodiac, the truly noble Leo, is a source of inspiration, a fountain of energy, a person of distinct generosity and kindness. It is this kind of Leo whose sun casts no shadows but burns brightly to bring light, heat, and warmth to everyone and everything around him.

The Leo List

Ruling planet: Sun
Gemstones: Cat's eye, ruby
Metal: Gold
Plants, herbs, and flowers: Anise, chamomile, daffodil, eyebright, fennel, lavender, yellow lily, poppy, marigold, mistletoe, parsley
Day of the week: Sunday
Numbers: 1 and 9
Color: Orange
Element: Fire
Quality: Fixed
Parts of the body: Back, heart, spinal column, spinal cord
Psychological characteristics and keywords: Assertive, enterprising, warm, affectionate, courageous, radiant, individualistic, demonstrative, creative, passionate, vain, domineering, falsely modest, arrogant, overwhelming, dictatorial, extravagant, braggart
Professions: Actor, artist, athlete, executive, pioneer, government official, head coach, foreman
Primary principle: Creativity
Biggest virtue: Compassion
Biggest flaw: Pride
Best signs for relationships: Sagittarius, Aries, Gemini, Libra
Spiritual impulse: The will to create
Famous Leo individuals: Henry Ford, Carl Jung, Jerry Garcia, Madonna, Jacqueline Kennedy Onassis, Bill Clinton, Mae West, Mick Jagger, Lucille Ball, Fidel Castro

VIRGO—THE VIRGIN
AUGUST 24–SEPTEMBER 22

 I Serve, Therefore I Am

Virgo's time of year comes during the summer harvest. The crops have ripened under the full heat of the Leo sun and are now ready for cultivation. Virgo is an earth sign. She is also called a "mutable" sign, one which gives a person many skills to cope successfully with all of life's challenges. Virgo comes into life with a "toolbox." It is filled with many different methods, techniques, and processes to reap the rewards from life's bounty and Virgo's own endeavors.

Most Virgos are very hard-working. They know that soon the colder months of the year will come. It will then be important to have a storehouse of material goods to keep her and her loved ones warm and secure. The way she handles her resources is a major issue to Virgo. She knows that she must maintain a clear head and cultivate perfect judgment in all that she says and does in order to ensure her security.

In this respect, there are many Virgos who can be too preoccupied about their personal and financial well-being and their material place in the world. Virgo is very job-conscious. She is always on the lookout for that additional opportunity, that perfect, secure niche in which to take refuge and be protected from life's harsher realities.

Virgo's mutability and incredibly active mind keep her always on the move, shifting and changing her views and perspectives. Like her Gemini brothers and sisters, Virgo is ruled by Mercury, the mental planet. Thus she tends to be far more mind-oriented than emotionally centered. In this respect, she will try to figure out or rationalize her emotions, creating practical reasons for why she should or should not feel a certain way. Her highly analytical mind gives her a very critical attitude about life. Virgo can find a fault in your logic as easily as she can spot a tiny hole in your sock!

If she is critical about others, Virgo is especially judgmental about herself. She is always looking for perfection, and this is especially true in her relationships. Virgo can hold herself back from personal involvements for what may seem to be a very long time until that "right" person comes along. This is not to say that Virgo never makes mistakes about people, but she usually takes great care in her choice of partners. Virgo likes to be a helpmate. She wants a person who has a sensible head on his shoulders and the possibility of a solid future in the making. Virgo likes to give of herself but she has to be sure that the other person is worthy of her many talents and loyal efforts.

Virgo requires that she be treated in a special way. She may not tell you what that way is (which can be rather confusing for the other person), but she will get very upset if you do not respect her particular code of behavior. Her keen judgment and critical assessments can be very helpful in the many practical issues of life. She does have to be careful, however, not to be too severe and impatient with others. If she takes a real hard look at the situation, she may just find that what bothers her most about someone else is really something within herself that she would like to see changed.

Food, diet, and health are also important to Virgo. Virgos can be very fussy about what and how they eat. This is only natural, as Virgo rules the digestive system in general and the intestines in particular. Whenever Virgo gets worried, her mental anxiety upsets her stomach and bowels. If the mind is troubled, food should not be taken into the body. This is true for all of the signs, but it is especially the case for Virgo. Yet the more mature and wise Virgo has an inner guide to when and what she should or should not consume. She will avoid over-indulgence of any kind and in fact be very helpful to others about their own physical health. For this reason, Virgos often find themselves in the role of nurse or doctor, for they are, after all, the healers of the zodiac.

The Virgo List

Ruling planet: Mercury

Gemstones: Citrine, yellow sapphire

Metal: Quicksilver

Plants, herbs, and flowers: Endive, millet, corn, wheat, barley, oats, rye, valerian, woodbine

Day of the week: Wednesday

Number: 6

Colors: Deep yellows and browns, yellowish-green

Element: Earth

Quality: Mutable

Parts of the body: Abdomen, intestines, abdominal cavity, spleen

Psychological characteristics and keywords: Organized, structured, helpful, unassuming, dependable, precise, meticulous, grounded, opinionated, obsessive, prudish, overly conservative, superficial, narrow-minded, critical

Professions: Nurse, doctor, service-oriented fields, accountant, secretary, veterinarian, librarian, statistician, psychiatrist, scientist

Primary principle: Discrimination

Biggest virtue: Clarity

Biggest flaw: Criticism

Best signs for relationships: Capricorn, Taurus, Cancer, Scorpio

Spiritual impulse: The will to refine judgment

Famous Virgo individuals: Ken Kesey, Oliver Stone, Lily Tomlin, Raquel Welch, Lauren Bacall, Sophia Loren, Leonard Bernstein, Sean Connery, Leo Tolstoy, Leonard Cohen

LIBRA—THE SCALES
SEPTEMBER 23–OCTOBER 23

 I Unite, Therefore I Am

Libra is always at work trying to balance opposites. Like his Taurus sisters, Libra is ruled by the goddess of love, Venus. Venus is known for her attributes of beauty and harmony. Although Libra is definitely a sign who searches for and aspires to peace, he can only come to that gentle state of being, to that greater sense of unity, through the resolution of conflict.

It is for this reason that we see a basic duality in Libra's life. On the one hand, Libra is ready to compromise at any cost (usually that cost is his own integrity). On the other hand, Libra is totally aware of conflict and works hard to find a solution to these differences so that everyone, including himself, may benefit. The wise Libran knows that it is only possible to have wholeness when each individual is aware of the other. This often happens as a result of a battle, successfully negotiated and truly resolved.

Libra is the most relationship-oriented sign of the zodiac. As an air sign, Libra has to communicate, and what Libra likes to communicate most are messages from Venus. Venus rules the romantic impulse in all of us. She is the planet of love. Instead of arguments, Venus offers poetry and music. In the place of misery, Venus gives princes and princesses courting each other in flower gardens. Venus is light and gentle, but too much of her influence in a horoscope can cause laziness and impracticality.

Libra has to beware his tendency to put off or avoid what seems uncomfortable. He can be very flighty and airy, denying personal responsibilities, preferring instead to wander through life with only temporary and superficial solutions to problems. Libra can develop a dreamlike attitude and may work hard at protecting his fairy castles, only to find that there are no real people inside them.

Libra is the born romantic searching for the ideal love relationship. He will feel extremely guilty if he is the cause of any interpersonal disturbance. If such a conflict does happen, Libra will not feel 100 percent right with himself until that situation is resolved both to his own and the other person's satisfaction.

Libra is always looking for a lover (and finding them too!). Once he is in such a relationship, Libra strives to make this union a perfect one. Yet perfection in relationship takes two: two people, two visions, two life goals, and two dreams. Some Librans suffer from a philosophy that states: "Be cooperative and do things my way!" Libra wants to share but may have difficulties with the give and take. Libra wants to join but may find that it's easier for another to join him than vice versa. All of these relationship complexities

are just parts of the Libran challenge in life: to give of himself without losing himself in the giving. He may also have to learn to accept another person without manipulating that person into Libra's ideal image.

Should Libra find himself in an unwanted relationship, he frequently has a difficult time untangling himself. He is instinctively adverse to split-ups. Remember, Libra is the sign of marriage; it is definitely not the sign of divorce. He will give the relationship every possible chance, but once he decides that he can no longer be in it, he has a special method of release. What Libra usually does is create a series of situations that can be so stressful that the other person initiates the break-up.

Naturally not all Librans walk with their feet in the clouds, focusing all their time and energy on their love life. Libra is also the sign of social justice and the law. Many Librans are dedicated to such issues as human rights and development of political freedom for the oppressed people of the world. Mahatma Gandhi was a Libra and so is Jimmy Carter. Libra is a visionary. His is a world of higher possibilities and refined values. Venus makes his powers of attraction very potent. He can thus bring many people to his social causes, uniting forces so that larger issues may be addressed.

As an air sign ruled by Venus, Libra functions from a very lofty point of view. It is true that some Librans' feet never touch the ground. But the majority of Librans have an instinct about correct conduct and right human relationships. This is an inner knowing which Libra can communicate to others, bringing in wonderful creative possibilities not only between himself and that one special person but among all people everywhere.

The Libra List

Ruling planet: Venus
Gemstones: Opal, carnelian
Metals: Copper, brass
Plants, herbs, and flowers: Watercress, strawberry, many types of vines, balm, violets, lemon thyme, white rose, primrose.
Day of the week: Friday
Number: 7
Colors: Green, bright yellow, white
Element: Air
Quality: Cardinal
Parts of the body: Loins; kidneys, appendix
Psychological characteristics and keywords: Balanced, refined, artistic, friendly, sociable, gregarious, charming, diplomatic, indecisive, self-indulgent, co-dependent, flighty, superficial
Professions: Lawyer, judge, marriage counselor, diplomat, decorator, musician, artist
Primary principle: Balance
Biggest virtue: Diplomacy
Biggest flaw: Indecisiveness
Best signs for relationships: Aquarius, Gemini, Sagittarius, Leo
Spiritual impulse: The will to unity
Famous Libra individuals: Mahatma Gandhi, John Lennon, Bob Weir, Mickey Mantle, Brigitte Bardot, Gore Vidal, Oscar Wilde, Chuck Berry, Timothy Leary, Barbara Walters

SCORPIO—THE SCORPION
OCTOBER 24–NOVEMBER 32

♏︎ *I Desire, Therefore I Am*

Scorpio loves secrecy. She has a special ability to penetrate into the center of another person's being and find out what that person is feeling. If she is your friend, you should have no fear that Scorpio will betray you, for she is very loyal to the people she loves. Yet as much as Scorpio finds it easy to understand the deepest parts of other people's lives, she has a difficult time revealing herself. You can tell Scorpio anything and everything. Expect her to keep your secret, but don't expect her to share her own.

Scorpio is the most intense sign of the zodiac. People born under her influence are known to live under a great deal of inner tension and internal pressure. Why is this so? What gives Scorpio a reputation of such mystery? Why are there so many people who find it easy to misunderstand this sign and yet are so attracted and fascinated by it? The answers to these questions may be found in two words: sex and death, the two areas of life under Scorpio's particular rulership.

Both sex and death are aspects of yet another quality of life: transformation. Scorpio's time of year occurs at the middle of autumn. This is when vegetation dies and decays. Yet the Earth and the trees are nourished by the debris of these fallen leaves and dead plants. Scorpio's strength lies in her ability to gather the power and potency from death so that new life may flourish at springtime. You may recall that Aries is the first sign of spring. Aries and Scorpio are brother and sister signs, as they are both ruled by the same planets, Mars and Pluto. What dies in in the fall of Scorpio is reborn in the spring of Aries.

Scorpio must continuously create transformation and change in her own life in order to grow. She is usually tested in this respect, as her inner power can only come forth once she has undergone the tension and test of surrender. Yet Scorpio resists change, has a fear of transformation, and usually uses her will to fight any outer or inner influence that tries to change her. She will even fight against herself. Yet she must yield to her own greater good, enter into a deep personal battle, and let go of what (or who!) is holding her back. Once she emerges from this conflict, she will be refreshed by her new life energy and ready to be more creative than ever before. Scorpio must die many times during her life so that she may live brighter and better. Scorpio represents reincarnation, and a good symbol for her and this process of death and rebirth is the caterpillar changing into the butterfly.

Scorpio's profound creative abilities can also emerge through the process of death and transformation. Scorpio is

the artist who makes a beautiful collage out of garbage, the sculptor who finds bits and pieces of discarded metal in the streets and uses them for an incredible work of art, or the musician who discovers a forgotten symphony in a music library and reworks it into a triumph. Scorpio is the healer working with a stroke patient, revitalizing that person's nervous system so that dead limbs may move again. Scorpio is the psychologist working with victims of abuse, giving them new hope so that they may love themselves again.

Sex is the other major area of Scorpio's life. Sex is the power and the vehicle allowing one generation to birth the next. Sex is the force that when correctly used brings the potent beauty of love into our lives on deep emotional, physical, and spiritual levels. Yet when sex is used incorrectly, it is an invitation to degeneration and death.

Some Scorpios are afraid of sex, death, and transformation. They bottle up the tensions of their fears and the intensity of their natural urges deep within themselves. Such people are bothered by deep emotional problems which they express through depression and anger. Most Scorpios recognize the harmonious power and wonderful beauty that sex shared lovingly can bestow. They can use their deep understanding of the sexual process for healing their human relationships. Many Scorpios are also capable of expressing their sexual energy in non-sexual ways through their creative and spiritual lives.

Scorpio can be a great helper and healer to anyone who lets her work her magic. It is a magic of deep emotional understanding and one which serves to bring another person to higher levels. In order to do this, Scorpio has to release what must be surrendered, transforming herself into what needs to be reborn.

The Scorpio List

Ruling planets: Pluto, Mars

Gemstones: Deep topaz, garnet

Metals: Plutonium, steel

Plants, herbs, and flowers: Bramble, heather, charlock, horehound, leak, wormwood, bean, blackthorn

Day of the week: Tuesday

Number: 8

Color: Dark red

Element: Water

Quality: Fixed

Parts of the body: Ovaries, bladder, prostate, testicles, colon, rectum

Psychological characteristics and keywords: Mysterious, deep, loyal, strong-willed, healing, regenerating, protective, sustaining, destructive, secretive, seductive, covert, manipulative, fearful, controlling, domineering

Professions: Surgeon, psychotherapist, investment banker, metaphysician, healer, investigator, detective, lawyer, chemist, soldier, undertaker

Primary principles: Death and rebirth

Biggest virtue: Regeneration

Biggest flaw: Abuse of power

Best signs for relationships: Cancer, Pisces, Virgo, Capricorn

Spiritual impulse: Will to transform

Famous Scorpio individuals: Prince Charles, Hillary Clinton, Stephen Hawking, Marie Curie, Indira Gandhi, Georgia O'Keeffe, Pablo Picasso, Meg Ryan, Rock Hudson

SAGITTARIUS—THE ARCHER
NOVEMBER 22–DECEMBER 21

 I Seek, Therefore I Am

"I see my goal. I reach my goal. And then I see another." These three short sentences should be the motto for Sagittarius. Known in astrology as the Centaur, a mythological creature who is half-man and half-horse, this great archer's arrows are filled with incredible creative powers.

Like his mythological counterpart, the Sagittarian individual is highly charged, eager for adventure, and always on the move. He is especially fond of travel and in fact has a difficult time ever staying still! He is a very restless soul, in constant pursuit of his dream. An idealistic person by nature, one of the greatest challenges for a Sagittarian is having to balance the ideal with the real. Sagittarius often believes that the future will be exactly the way he can see it in his mind. He has a much harder time working through the logistics of life on Earth in order to turn that dream into a physical reality. Although there are certainly many Sagittarians willing to do what is necessary to achieve their goals, there are just as many who are not particularly geared to physical struggles. These individuals would rather talk about their inner visions than do something about creating them. If we search a bit deeper into mythology, we find that the Centaur's mother was the Earth goddess, Gaia. It is therefore important for Sagittarius to find his place on our planet. Once he does assume the practical responsibility for his vision, his dreams may turn into the reality he hopes for.

Sagittarius is the luckiest sign in the zodiac. He is ruled by Jupiter, the kindest and most benevolent of all the planets. Expansive and generous by nature, happy and cheerful in character, Sagittarius is liked by others and he likes them. Sagittarius is "jovial." This word comes from the name the Romans gave to Jupiter, Jove. The Romans could party on and on; so can Sagittarius! Parties and good times are very much a favorite pastime for our Centaur friends. Sagittarians bring joy into people's lives, showing others of a more limited or depressed imagination that life is full of amazing possibilities if you can only imagine them.

It is not surprising, then, that Sagittarius is called the "philosopher of the zodiac," for his basic nature is to teach and instruct. He likes nothing more than to show others how to get things done. His methods are not the practical ones of the more earthy signs (Taurus, Virgo, and Capricorn). His techniques are all in the realm of ideas.

Sagittarius can teach you how to open your mind to your wider possibilities. He can give you certain insights into life that expand your vision to such an extent that there is no problem you can't solve. Sagittarius' astrological symbol is the arrow. It is an arrow pointed ever upwards towards the heavens. In this same way, Sagittarius is always looking optimistically ahead toward the next field of endeavor, the next realm of accomplishment, the next possibility of achievement.

As the philosopher-teacher, Sagittarius is always talking, and his usual tone of voice is anything but subtle. Sagittarius is known to suffer from an acute case of "foot-in-mouth disease." His blunt way of expressing himself is often shocking and shattering to others who prefer a less head-on confrontation with life. Sagittarius is truthful by nature (and sometimes a bit rude!). He just cannot understand why other people are not as up-front about things as he is.

Sagittarius has a hard time with emotional subtleties in relationships. Consequently, his best partners for relationships are usually not people who have strong placements in the water signs (Cancer, Scorpio, and Pisces).

Sagittarius is definitely not a "clinger." He wants relationships that are bold and adventurous, not confined by intense emotional demands or pressures. He is definitely passionate and romantic, but this passion and romanticism are best expressed when he is on vacation! Sagittarius must be free to roam and wander. This does not necessarily mean that he has to be or is sexually promiscuous. It does mean, however, that he has to know that he has the personal freedom to explore his own life and to come back to share with his loved ones what he has learned.

The Sagittarius List

Ruling planet: Jupiter
Gemstones: Amethyst, turquoise
Metal: Tin
Day of the week: Thursday
Number: 9
Color: Purple
Element: Fire
Quality: Mutable
Parts of the body: Hips, thighs, lower vertebrae, sacral region, sciatic nerves
Psychological characteristics and keywords: Enthusiastic, generous, independent, inspirational, optimistic, courageous, straightforward, sarcastic, fanatical, unrealistic, overzealous, obnoxious, exaggerated, gluttonous, unsatisfied
Professions: Philosopher, professor (humanities), publisher, navigator, judge, athlete, philanthropist, teacher, minister, orator, promoter
Primary principle: Exploration
Biggest virtue: Wisdom
Biggest flaw: Delusion
Best signs for relationships: Leo, Aries, Libra, Aquarius
Spiritual impulse: Will to expanded awareness
Famous Sagittarius individuals: Jimi Hendrix, Jim Morrison, Ludwig van Beethoven, Mark Twain, Steven Spielberg, Walt Disney, Harpo Marx, Dick Clark, Woody Allen, Bette Midler

CAPRICORN—THE MOUNTAIN GOAT
DECEMBER 22–JANUARY 20

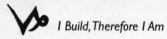 *I Build, Therefore I Am*

Capricorn's position in the zodiac is at the top of the astrological wheel. This is an appropriate placement for her, as Capricorn is the Mountain Goat, climbing ever upwards towards the fulfillment of her many goals. No other sign is as capable of sustaining the pressures and responsibilities of success as is Capricorn. And no other sign can be as fearful of falling down from her pinnacle as is the Mountain Goat.

Capricorn may often begin life in difficult circumstances, but she usually ends it in ease and comfort. Her family may be emotionally troublesome for her, and she may find that she has too much responsibility at too young an age. As she grows up, the demands of society and the need to find a suitable profession can at first be oppressive. Once she finds her place, however, she can transform her anxiety into creative ambition.

Yet Capricorn has been called the "worrier of the zodiac." Her need is to be in control; her fear is being controlled. She can get very upset when she feels that her will is not the ultimate influence in her surroundings. Capricorn seeks to build upon every idea, profit from every venture, and gain in a material or spiritual sense from each one of her experiences. It is no wonder then that Capricorn is the sign which rules big business, governments, corporations and their respective CEOs, premiers, and executives. More presidents of the United States have had either their Moon or Sun in Capricorn at birth than in any other sign!

With each promotion in life comes a new level of responsibility. In this respect, Capricorns often have a love-hate relationship with what they achieve. A Capricorn cannot stay at the bottom rung of any ladder for too long. She has too much drive, too much ambition. Her sense of personal obligation is also very strong, and she easily feels limited, hemmed in, and restricted by life. She knows that she must move forward, but with each step along her way, she encounters more challenges.

Capricorn usually responds in one of two ways to this dilemma. Either she continues to stay in her little corner, anchoring her feet deeper and deeper until the sense of limitation overwhelms her, or she finds the inner courage to move forward, climb to the next level in life, and assume the responsibilities that await her. In this case, she has to bring to her new situation an even greater sense of personal authority and self-definition.

Capricorns have an interesting approach to relationships. Some Mountain Goats are notorious social climbers, choosing partners that will further their position within their social group or business. Sentimentality and romance matter less in these cases than money, prestige, and power. We have to remember that Capricorn is an earthy sign; as such, the material aspects of life mean a great deal to her.

Other Capricorns are incredibly supportive, choosing partners who may not have achieved a high social position but are willing to go there. These Mountain Goats are going to climb high, and they are going to take their loved ones with them! One thing is for certain, Capricorn will avoid someone without ambition and drive—a person without vision and courage need not apply at Capricorn's office or home for a job!

One of the key astrological phrases for Capricorn is "I use." The Mountain Goat is acutely aware of the material and social circumstances in her environment and is not beyond manipulating what she sees for her own benefit. In this respect some Capricorns may sacrifice friendship for ambition. Yet there is another kind of Capricorn called the "Sea Goat." The Sea Goat swims in the waters of human compassion and is aware of the struggles of other people. This Capricorn uses her will, drive, strength, job, or social position to help others and free them from their material and spiritual boundaries and limitations. The Sea Goat has produced such people as Martin Luther King, Jr., Albert Schweitzer, and Joan of Arc.

The Capricorn List

Ruling planet: Saturn
Gemstones: Dark sapphires, jet, obsidian
Metal: Lead
Day of the week: Saturday
Number: 4
Colors: Indigo, grey
Element: Earth
Quality: Cardinal
Parts of the body: Knees, skeletal system, joints, teeth
Psychological characteristics and keywords: Prudent, enduring, patient, organized, structured, stable, industrious, productive, persistent, miserly, obstinate, unsympathetic, overly conservative, dictatorial, insatiably ambitious, opportunistic
Professions: Politician, banker, manager, real-estate broker, architect, government official
Primary principle: Order
Biggest virtue: Accomplishment
Biggest flaw: Opportunistic
Best signs for relationships: Virgo, Taurus, Scorpio, Pisces
Spiritual impulse: The will to integrate the higher and lower selves
Famous Capricorn individuals: Nostradamus, David Bowie, Mao Tse-tung, Elvis Presley, Martin Luther King, Jr., Janis Joplin, Joan of Arc, Edgar Allan Poe, Marlene Dietrich, Richard Nixon

AQUARIUS—THE HUMAN
JANUARY 20–FEBRUARY 18

 I Aspire, Therefore I Am

Aquarius has a most interesting reputation among astrologers. The "bohemian of the zodiac" is often quite unconventional. At the very least, he hates any rules but his own, and he is known to change such rules to suit his immediate needs. You cannot predict what an Aquarian will do next, and neither can he!

Aquarius is an air sign. Air likes to circulate, and Aquarius likes to circulate in some very unusual places with some very unusual people! The Aquarian is a social experimenter. He is especially fond of being with people who, like himself, are not conventional in their behavior. The group is important to him, and friendship is a vital facet of his life. He is idealistic and would like to see a world of equality and freedom for all people. These are definitely the characteristics found in a large number of our Aquarian brothers and sisters, those ruled by that eccentric and highly idealistic planet, Uranus.

Aquarius is one of four signs that has two planetary rulers (the others are Aries, Scorpio, and Pisces). The other group of Aquarians is influenced more by Saturn. These individuals are only attracted to people who believe as they do. Their group loyalties are reserved for those who are just like themselves. The Uranus-ruled Aquarians seek to be different to such an extent that they may shun all forms of group activity, thinking that joining with anyone else is compromising their own identity! The Saturn-ruled Aquarian likes the sense of group responsibility and ordered, structured, collective activities. At the same time, the Saturn-ruled Aquarian seeks a powerful leader, a person who is the embodiment of what the group stands for, believes in, and represents. This Aquarian has a shallow sense of himself and feels much more comfortable being told what to do and what to believe. He therefore finds himself drawn to political and/or religious cults or groups with extreme views. This connection takes away the burden of having to make his own decisions and create his own activities.

The Saturn-ruled Aquarian is quite the contrast to the more developed, Uranus-ruled Aquarian, who is generally possessed with a wide understanding of the possibilities life has to offer. He is involved with the future and with putting his actions and beliefs to work for him. He often associates with those groups and organizations of a more humanitarian and socially progressive nature as he seeks social equality and liberation from oppression.

Until an Aquarian matures from an idealist to a person who is out in the world actually creating the changes he envisions, he may find that the ideal is stronger than the real. As an airy, mental sign, he has to take care that his ideas

are not more important than their execution and that his mind is not too far ahead of his body. Some Aquarians may easily lose track of their feet because their head is in the clouds. A mature Aquarian, on the other hand, brings insight, vision, and great originality to any situation. He is aware of the new, an excellent judge of human nature, and precise in his intuitive approach to life.

Some Aquarians may have a difficult time prioritizing their activities. They are so creative mentally that they can conceive of numerous projects at the same time but may have considerable difficulty choosing which one should come first. The same is true in terms of friendships. Aquarius is an especially friendly sign who enjoys the company of others. Yet he may easily lose sight of the relative importance of relationships. To an Aquarian, a lover may be just another friend. This can make it difficult for the other person if he or she is born under a sign whose emotional priorities are certain (such as Aries, Cancer or Leo). Yet this same tendency towards equality gives Aquarius an inner sense of fair play regardless of personal considerations.

As a friend or a lover, Aquarius is very loyal—in his fashion! He requires a great deal of personal freedom. He usually has a wide circle of friends but few intimates. He needs to be able to move openly within his social group, sometimes alone and sometimes with his partner. The best person for an Aquarian is another independent individual, one who is free of the need to stay close all the time. Aquarians can be very, very aloof and detached, and they can be this way at the most intimate of moments. Of course, Aquarians are capable of romance, but first and foremost an Aquarian is a friend. If the joy and cooperation of friendship are what you require in a relationship, if you are attracted by the new and different, the unusual and the fascinating, then Aquarius is definitely your sign for relationship. If it is possessive, passionate intensity that you are seeking, you had better look elsewhere (try Scorpio or Leo).

The Aquarius List

Ruling planets: Uranus, Saturn
Gemstone: Light blue sapphires
Metals: Radium, uranium
Plants, herbs, and flowers: Frankincense, myrrh
Day of the week: Saturday
Number: 11
Colors: Violet, indigo, azure
Element: Air
Quality: Fixed
Parts of the body: Ankles, legs, the circulatory systems in general, and blood circulation in particular
Psychological characteristics and keywords: Social, friendly, objective, conceptual, theoretical, intuitive, inclusive, inquisitive, pioneering, unfocused, egotistical, erratic, aloof, detached, unpredictable, impractical, over-intellectual, ungrounded
Professions: Humanitarian, explorer, musician, astrologer, electrician, psychologist, radio technician, computer scientist, astronomer, inventor, political and social activist
Primary principle: Change
Biggest virtue: Originality
Biggest flaw: Rebelliousness
Best signs for relationships: Gemini, Libra, Sagittarius, Aries
Spiritual impulse: The will to evolve
Famous Aquarius individuals: Charles Darwin, Babe Ruth, Wolfgang Amadeus Mozart, Gertrude Stein, Ronald Reagan, Abraham Lincoln, Mia Farrow, Yoko Ono, John Travolta, Carole King

PISCES—THE FISH
FEBRUARY 19–MARCH 20

 I Understand, Therefore I Am

As the last sign of the zodiac, Pisces has characteristics of all the preceding eleven plus its own special nature as well. This means that Pisces is the most compassionate and empathic of all the signs. She is usually willing and able to hear other people's troubles, offering support and comfort. On the other hand, Pisces' sense of herself can be severely challenged by other people, and the Fish may find herself lost in the emotional waters of other "swimmers."

This is but one of many dualities belonging to this highly sensitive and complex sign. The symbol of the Fish represents the basic duality of her life: two fish swimming in opposite directions. One of the fish swims upstream. This indicates the Piscean urge to the spiritual life, to an understanding of the invisible, to the need to sacrifice herself in unselfish ways for the benefit of others.

The other fish swims downstream. This represents the more difficult side of the Piscean nature: the urge for self-destruction. Pisces is known to pull the rug out from under her own feet on more than one occasion. She can often write her name on the blackboard with one hand and erase it simultaneously with the other. In other words, she has a difficult time giving herself a distinct sense of personal identification. Each time she approaches the discipline and boundaries so necessary for a successful life, whether in business or romance, she swims in another direction—often away from her envisioned goal.

Pisces has a fear of confinement, containment, and restriction. Once she overcomes this fear with a sense of commitment to her own abundant creative potential, then there are few restraints to hold her back from any accomplishment.

One of the most beautiful things about Pisces is her fluidity and grace. She seems to be able to glide through life without causing any waves. She brings soothing harmony, beauty, and joy wherever she goes—and she goes to many places! Pisces is one of the mutable (or movable) signs of the zodiac. It is this inner changeability, a natural restlessness, which creates in her the urge for exploration and adventure.

Actually, there are three types of Pisces. The first is the "minnow." This is a little nervous fish who is carried through life by the waves and currents of her environment. She seems to have no direction of her own and lives in a constant state of agitation and fear. The second is the "dolphin." This is the Pisces who is the embodiment of the arts.

She is the ballet dancer, the photographer, the actress, the costume designer. She moves through life with effortless grace, in touch with her special muse. The third is the "whale." This is often, as the name implies, a large person, sometimes in body, always in spirit. The Pisces whale is at work helping others. Even if not a healer or social worker (and many of them are just that), the attitude of the Pisces whale is "What can I do to help you?"

Pisces is known to be attracted to two types of relationships, depending on which direction the Fish is swimming. The downstream fish is attracted to people who are harmful to her and who take advantage of Pisces' material and emotional resources. The upstream fish relates to very sensitive, creative people. She connects with those individuals whose nature is rather spiritual insofar as they, like herself, are leading their lives in the hopes of performing some service of goodwill in the world.

The part of the body ruled by the Fish is the feet. The feet are the only part of ourselves in constant contact with the Earth. They absorb the vital energies of nature and connect us to our understanding about life. In this respect, Pisces is in touch with all possible forms of human emotional response. She is a person of deep and far-reaching feeling. Once Pisces learns to respect and then master her own highly sensitive nature, once she is able to create a field of service which allows her to use that sensitivity wisely, then the two Fish may swim upstream together.

The Pisces List

Ruling planets: Jupiter, Neptune
Gemstones: Deep amethyst, blue topaz
Metals: Lithium, platinum
Plants, herbs, and flowers: Seaweed, ferns, mosses, water lilies, lotus, and all other plants that grow in the water
Day of the week: Thursday
Number: 22
Colors: Deep violet, sea green, blue-violet
Element: Water
Quality: Mutable
Part of the body: Feet
Psychological characteristics and keywords: Selfless, compassionate, receptive, imaginative, flowing, adaptive, unifying, psychic, disordered, undefined, hallucinatory, paranoid, powerless, untruthful, martyred
Professions: Actor, photographer, hair stylist, philosopher, mystic, clairvoyant, physician, poet, writer
Primary principle: Unity
Biggest virtue: Compassion
Biggest flaw: Martyrdom
Best signs for relationships: Scorpio, Cancer, Capricorn, Taurus
Spiritual impulse: The will to love unconditionally
Famous Pisces individuals: Rudolf Nureyev, Gloria Vanderbilt, Elizabeth Taylor, Albert Einstein, Billy Crystal, Drew Barrymore

The Houses

As you can see from the following diagram, the horoscope is divided into twelve primary sections, called "houses." These twelve houses are vitally important to understanding the way astrology works in your life. Practically everything we see around us, or associate with our daily lives, may be found in one or more of these house divisions. This chapter discusses the most important categories, subjects, people, and places found in each of these astrological domiciles.

We know from our reading of the previous two chapters that the planets represent the "whats" of the chart and the signs the "hows." Now we come to the "wheres." After memorizing the astrological symbols and reading about the houses of the horoscope, you can begin to put the whats, hows, and wheres together. You will then have some preliminary insights as to how to read a horoscope yourself. For example, you will see from this chapter that the fourth house has a great deal to do with the home. So if a person has Venus (relationships) in Libra (balance) in the fourth house, the tendency would be for that person to have balanced and harmonious relationships in her home. Just keep using the keywords and information found in your sign, planet, and house associations lists, and you will see that the great complexity of astrology (and life) will gradually reveal itself to you!

The houses of the horoscope are determined by the time and place of your birth. Unless you know these two factors, it will be impossible for you to determine your "Rising Sign" (see below) or any of the other signs that are on your house "cusps." These cusps are the actual twelve points of division of the 360 degrees of the zodiac that make up your individual horoscope. The signs on the cusps are very important and will tell you "how" the various events in your life are expressed.

You can easily find out your Rising Sign or any of the other eleven house cusps by having your horoscope cast by computer. Often, your local metaphysical bookstore will provide such a service at a nominal cost. You may even decide to go further into astrology yourself and purchase astrological software for your personal computer. In the "ancient days" (pre-1978!) before such software was developed, astrologers (including the writer of this book) had to compute the houses as well as the exact positions of the planets by hand. So welcome to the Age of Aquarius, my friends; you are very fortunate indeed.

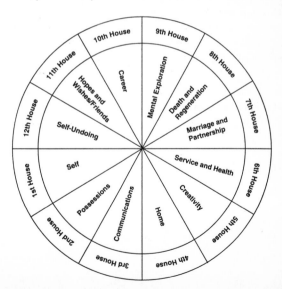

First House and the Ascendant

 This is probably the most important house in the chart (at least until a person is about twenty-nine, and then the tenth house becomes increasingly more important). The ascendant (or Rising Sign) is your projected image, the door through which you express your personality and its immediate needs into the environment. The ascendant also characterizes your physical appearance and gives others their first impression of you. For example, someone with Gemini rising is apt to be wiry and slender with a nervous disposition. A Sagittarius ascendant gives a large person with an optimistic attitude and an eagerness for adventure.

The first house is related to the sign Aries, the spring season, and the planet Mars. It is thus a place where the energies of life project themselves strongly and eagerly.

Keywords: personality, your projected image, the character mask you wear, the structure of your physical body, and your ego.

Second House

The second house is associated with the sign Taurus and the planet Venus. As such it is connected to the more material aspects of life. The second house holds and describes a great deal about our sense of self-worth, not just in terms of money but also in terms of everything that we value in life and ourselves. The second house acts much like our personal bank. It contains those resources that we use and project through the indications of our ascendant and the first house.

Keywords: practical security, finances, real estate, investment potential, possessions, personal values

Third House

This house deals with communications and immediate relationships. It is the house of Gemini and the planet Mercury. As such it involves short journeys (those lasting one day or less), or a series of short journeys. It tells us about the nature of our early environment and/or our everyday environment. Thus we find our brothers, sisters, neighbors, and close friends described by this house of our horoscope. As a communications house, the third characterizes your natural mental abilities and intellectual capacities.

Keywords: personal ideas, education (to high school level), brief travels, the rational mind and its development, immediate family (but not parents)

Fourth House

This deals with our psychological foundations. It is the natural house of the sign Cancer and its ruler, the Moon. As such, the fourth deals with our most subjective qualities and has a great deal to do with our instinctive patterns of behavior, as it describes our life before the age of seven. The fourth is the first house of summer. It tells us much about our "roots," and like the plants in the earth, it speaks to us about our psychological soil and the familial nutriments that either allow us to flower or stunt our growth.

The fourth house is traditionally associated with our mother, our biological gene pool, and our domestic situation in general. For example, if a person were to have Taurus on the cusp of their fourth house, he or she would tend to want a home filled with comforts and material security and would definitely not like to move around a great deal, as Taurus is a very fixed sign. A water sign like Pisces on the cusp of the fourth would give a person the inclination to live near the ocean or by a lake. Pisces on the fourth can also indicate one who has a deeply sensitive and compassionate nature.

Keywords: psychological foundations, mother's influence, sense of inner security, domestic issues

Fifth House

 As the natural home of the Sun and its sign, Leo, the fifth is concerned with the outward expression of our talents and capabilities. It is the house of art and is especially associated with pleasure. One of the most important creative possibilities we have is our ability to have children. Thus young people and one's relationship with them are part of the fifth house scenario. Romance is also a fifth house issue. In fact, the fifth is called the "house of lovers." It is not the house of partnership or marriage (that, as we shall soon see, belongs to the seventh), but it is that area in our chart which speaks about love affairs. The fifth also deals with games and speculation. People who gamble with love and/or money are very likely to have a strong fifth house in their natal chart.

Keywords: creativity, courtship and romance, children, the pleasures of life

Sixth House

This is another house ruled by that very busy planet Mercury. The sign most closely aligned to this area of your life is Virgo. As such, the sixth has a great deal to do with those methods, techniques, and processes you use for work. The goal of the sixth house is to provide the tools we need to perfect ourselves, both materially and physically. It is therefore the house of health. An astrologer can tell a great deal about a person's physical state by examining the sixth house in a chart (plus looking at the nature of the Sun and Moon in the horoscope). In addition, the sixth has a lot to do with your pets and anyone who happens to work for you.

Keywords: service and labor, diet and health, tools and jobs, practical resources readily available to you

Seventh House

As the house associated with Libra and its ruling planet, Venus, you would expect the seventh to be very much involved with relationships. If the first house speaks exclusively about "you," then the seventh, which is exactly opposite the first, speaks about the "not-you." It tells what you are most attracted to in others and thus what you seek to incorporate into yourself to give you a sense of wholeness.

The "not-you" also speaks about what you may find that opposes you. In this respect, the seventh house speaks to us about opponents, enemies, and those kinds of relationships that may bring challenges into our lives. Business as well as intimate partners are also under the influence of this part of the natal chart. The nature of the seventh house is the most important factor when it comes to partnerships and your natural choice of relationship circumstances.

Keywords: relationships, rivals, partnerships of all kinds, opponents in lawsuits

Eighth House

If the second house of the horoscope represents your resources, the eighth house is representative of other people's resources in general and resources coming from partnerships in particular. As such, it is the house of alimony as well as income from mutual interests (such as royalties from a book, commissions from sales, etc.). It is also the house of death and as such it represents inheritances and legacies. Although much may be said about the nature of an individual's physical death through an examination of the eighth, this house also has a lot to do with psychological and spiritual death. It speaks about how we may "die" to one stage of life or to one phase of our emotional development and then be reborn into our next step.

This house is under the natural rulership of Scorpio and its two planetary rulers, Mars and Pluto. No wonder, then, that another major lesson found within the borders of the eighth has to do with sex. It is through this house that the astrologer can determine one's natural sexual orientation as well as those events that occur in our life that involve sexual issues.

Keywords: sex, death, inheritance, partner's finances, spiritual and physical regeneration, dreams, occult studies

Ninth House

This is the home of Jupiter and the sign Sagittarius. As such, it is in the ninth house that we find our tendencies for long-distance travel, higher education, religion, and philosophy. As this is the third house from the seventh, the ninth deals with your partner's relatives (your in-laws) plus distant family members. The ninth is also the house related to collective knowledge. If you have important astrological placements in this house, you are very likely to be a history buff and be open to such pursuits as archaeology, foreign languages, and publishing. This is the area in the horoscope that relates to social conduct and morals. Thus we find that the law and justice come under its influence. An astrologer can see your relationship to the legal system (lawsuits, etc.) through study of this area of the natal chart.

Keywords: religion, philosophy, higher education, long-distance journeys, legal issues

Tenth House

This house is extremely important, falling under the influence of Saturn and Capricorn. The cusp of this house is called the "Midheaven"; abbreviated as M.C. for the Latin word (*medius coeli*). The M.C. speaks of a person's career and place in society. If you were to have Aries on this cusp, you would most likely be self-employed or involved in a pioneering career. You find people in authoritarian positions in the tenth, and it is traditionally known as the house of the father. It would therefore describe your father's character, even his sign, and tell us much about your relationship with him. If we were to compare your fourth house with your tenth, we would know a great deal about your parents and their relationship. The tenth is the first house of winter, and like the cold weather, tells us how you consolidate your energy and bring focus to your creativity. It is here that we can determine the scope of a person's social contribution and his or her most likely career choices. The tenth is also a "money house" (like the second and the sixth) and reveals much about the results of your financial issues.

Keywords: professional life, community standing, goals, ability to handle responsibilities and personal authority

Eleventh House

This segment of the horoscope is under the influence of the sign Aquarius, the planet Uranus, and, secondarily, the planet Saturn. It speaks to us about a person's social connections and the general network of relationships one makes in life.

It is thus the house of friends and social acquaintances. The third house has more to do with those intimate friends we consider as brothers or sisters. It is through the activities of the eleventh that we express our hopes, wishes, and aspirations. Our creative talents (fifth house) are broadened in the eleventh so that whatever we produce is extended into society at large.

Keywords: social life, friends, companions, groups, income from career (second house from the tenth)

Twelfth House

This is probably the most mysterious house of the natal chart, ruled by Neptune (secondarily by Jupiter) and the sign Pisces. As such, we often find a great deal to do with the shadow side of our character. It is the house of hidden enemies, or those aspects of our personality which work against our best interest. The twelfth is also the house of clandestine relationships, secret love affairs, as well as hospitals, monasteries, and other places of retreat from the world.

The twelfth can be a very beneficial house. It is the place where our hidden resources and inner treasures are located. A strong Venus or Jupiter located in the twelfth house of our horoscope can give us money or a helping hand when we least expect it. This is the house of our spiritual treasures as well, and a positive twelfth house can lead to a life filled with amazing spiritual revelations and inner guidance.

Another name for the twelfth is the "House of Karma." If we believe in reincarnation, the twelfth house is the storage place of events and consequences from past lives. Regardless of our orientation to past lives, the twelfth shows us what we need to overcome in this life, as well as some of the power we possess deep within ourselves in order to accomplish this task.

Keywords: spiritual life, subconscious mind, hidden places, deepest and most profound gifts from life

To make the study of the houses a bit easier, we may classify them as follows:

Houses one, two, and three deal primarily with our personal life and our major personality traits (one), our money, values, and resources (two), and our ideas, opinions, and methods of communication (three).

Houses four, five, and six deal with our domestic life and speak about our family (four), children and talents (five), and our health, work skills, and attitudes (six).

Houses seven, eight, and nine are most concerned with our relationships in business and marriage (seven), to other people's money and resources (eight), and to higher education in order to advance our life intellectualy and socially (nine).

Houses ten, eleven, and twelve are involved with our larger social world and our impact on it through our career and social standing (ten), our friends and associates (eleven), and our urge to clean up our past and get on with our spiritual journey (twelve).

Interpreting the Horoscope

Astrology is both an art and a science. It is an evolving science as it is based upon a definite set of rules and principles proven effective over thousands of years of practice. Modern astrologers are constantly adding to our astrological understanding of life. Astrology is an art in the way each practitioner interprets the results of calculations of the heavenly positions. The art of the astrologer depends as much on intuitive perceptions as on accumulated knowledge and experience.

The usual oral interpretation of a chart can last from one to several hours, depending on what the client requests and the astrologer's way of responding. A written analysis of a natal chart can thus run from a few to dozens of pages.

What follows are two brief interpretations of the horoscopes of well known people. I have used only those essential elements of astrology presented in this book and have not included certain advanced techniques and methods that reveal the more subtle elements of the chart. These are by no means complete interpretations, but I hope that these "readings" will further spark your interest in an expanded investigation of astrology's potential.

You will be able to follow these interpretations more closely by referring back to those chapters dealing with the significance of the particular planets, signs, and houses. To help you out a little further, you will find some words and phrases in parentheses in the text of the interpretations. These are cross-references to give you additional insights into the meanings of astrological symbolism as we use it.

Prince Charles, born November 14, 1948, at 9:14 P.M., London, England:

Prince Charles has the Sun in Scorpio in the fourth house of his natal chart. This position indicates an intense and basically private person who has the roots of his power in his family and genealogical background. Although his Leo Ascendant (the sign of kings) shows a person who likes to have attention paid to him, his Scorpio Sun is indicative of a man who wants to keep his secrets. This combination of Scorpio and Leo reveals one of Prince Charles' basic conflicts: the need to be recognized, flattered, and publicly ceremonial (Leo), and his basic urge for secrecy, privacy, and introspection (Scorpio).

The Moon in this chart is in Taurus in the tenth house. The Taurus Moon shows a liking for physical comfort and material abundance. It indicates that his domestic life (Moon) will be very public (tenth house). It also reveals that his public standing (tenth) will come from his family, especially his mother (Moon). It is also interesting to note that Queen Elizabeth is a Taurus and her Sun is at the same degree of the zodiac as is her son's Moon. This shows a direct line of descent between mother and son in terms of the power and possessions of this family.

This conflict between Charles's public life and private life reveals itself in many other places in the chart. The Moon in a man's chart indicates his wife. Taurus is called the "honor sign" for the Moon, and its position in the "house of honor" (tenth) shows his marriage to the very popular and beautiful Princess Diana. In fact, their marriage ceremony was the most public in history, as it was broadcast all over the world. This is seen in the horoscope by the fact that Aquarius (public, large groups) is on the cusp of his seventh

Prince Charles

Sunday, November 14, 1948 21:14:00
London, England
Time Zone: 00:00 (UT)
Longitude 000° W 05'
Latitude 51° N 32'

house of marriage. The ruling planet of Aquarius, Uranus (television and other methods of communication) is in Prince Charles' eleventh house (broadcasting, humanity in general) in the sign of Gemini (communication, media, journalism). Yet the Prince always had a secret love. This is seen by Venus (romance) being so very close to Neptune (hidden things) in the sign of Libra (relationships) in the fourth house (subjective, inner life).

The Prince is a sportsman, as Jupiter (games) and Mars (competition and aggression) are in the fifth house (hobbies, pleasures). He is especially fond of polo (Jupiter rules large animals and is in Sagittarius, the sign of the Centaur—half-man, half-horse). He is also an enormously wealthy man. Leo is on the cusp of his second house of money and its ruler, the Sun, is in Scorpio (sign of inheritance) in the fourth house (family). He may inherit a kingdom and will certainly inherit a great fortune from his mother (fourth house, Moon in Taurus). But will he be king?

He has Pluto (death and rebirth) in his first house (personality). This gives Prince Charles very good recuperative powers, but it also means that the power of Pluto to his Scorpio Sun (more death than rebirth!) may be too much. It is quite possible that he may not be king at all. One thing for sure, his son will be a future king. His house of children (the fifth) is very fortunate because Jupiter (the great giver of good fortune) is in that house in its own sign. This shows that his son will rise to a place of honor and should be a strong and powerful monarch. But this power will be more philosophical than physical, as Mars, along with Jupiter, is in the fifth house in the "noble" sign of Sagittarius.

Jacqueline Kennedy Onassis, born July 28, 1929, at 2:30 P.M., Southampton, New York:

America's own "royal family" could certainly be said to include "Queen Jacqueline." Born under the royal sign of Leo, her Sun is placed in the ninth house of foreign travel. This is also the house of publishing, where Mrs. Onassis expressed herself strongly during the later part of her life. Mercury (writing and travel) is also in that house, giving this area of her life increased power.

She has Scorpio on the Ascendant, adding the magnetism, mystery, and mystique that was so much a part of her personality. Pluto, the ruler of this sign, is in the eighth house of regeneration and rebirth, demonstrating her power to be strong and continue after the assassination of John F. Kennedy. Her qualities of self-assertion, courage, and bravery are also seen by the placement of her Moon in the warrior sign of Aries. It is in her fifth house, which indicates her closeness to her children as well as her ability to apply form and focus to her own creative abilities.

It is interesting to note that Jupiter is in her seventh house of marriage in the sign of Gemini. This shows that both of her marriages were with men characterized by Jupiter's influence. JFK (who was a Gemini) was a communicator whose philosophy and public statements affected many people of his generation. Aristotle Onassis demonstrated the entrepreneurial side of Jupiter's nature, as did Jacqueline's long-time companion, Maurice Templesman, who was a wealthy financier. The wealth of all three men is seen by the sign Taurus on the cusp of her seventh house (relationships). Venus, the ruling planet of Taurus, is in the eighth house of partner's resources and reveals the financial legacy that she received from her husbands. This is accentuated by the placement of the Moon's Northern Node in Taurus on the seventh house cusp.

The combination of Scorpio rising (drive, determination, mystery, resourcefulness, regenerative power), the Sun in Leo (fixity, charisma, abundant creative power), and the Moon in Aries (courage, self-assurance, faith in one's own actions) certainly made for a woman who will remain a powerful figure in American and world history.

Jacqueline Kennedy Onassis

Sunday, July 28, 1929 14:30:00
Southampton, New York
Time Zone: 04:00 (EDT)
Longitude 072° W 23'
Latitude 40° N 53'

An Astrological Glossary

Astrology has a complete and interesting vocabulary. In fact, when astrologers get together, they speak a jargon that is largely incomprehensible to outsiders. It is, after all, a language which attempts to describe all the subtleties of human consciousness through its symbology and geometry. You could, for example, be giving your friend a long explanation about the complexities of your current relationship. You try to tell her that it is difficult for you to feel the difference between your emotions and those of your loved one. You go on to say that you are having some trouble understanding the level of intimacy you share, etc. If you and your friend were astrologers, all you would tell her would be: "My natal Moon square Neptune is at work again!" And your friend would simply reply, "I understand," and probably offer you some advice!

Following is a list of some of the more commonly used terms in the astrological "language." It is by no means complete, but it will add quite a bit of information to your current and future studies of this ancient science and perhaps stimulate your wanting to speak "astrologese" more fluently.

Ascendant: Also known as your "rising sign," the ascendant is the degree of the zodiac rising at the horizon at the time and place of your birth. Next to your sun and moon signs, the sign of your ascendant is the most important factor in your horoscope. It indicates a great deal about your personality and physical appearance.

Aspects: Astrologers can determine a great deal about the way the planetary forces operate in your life by measuring the number of degrees between the planets. Following are the most important of the geometric angles that can exist between the planets in the 360-degree circle of the zodiac of signs. (Each of the 12 signs in 30 degrees in length: 12x30=360.)

Conjunction: This occurs when planets occupy the same degree of a sign, (+ 8 degrees). If you had Mercury at 10 Scorpio and Venus at 15 Scorpio, we would say that you had a conjunction between Mercury and Venus. The conjunction adds intensity and power to the planets.

Opposition: This occurs when two planets are exactly opposite each other (180 degrees apart) + 8 degrees. If Venus were at 6 Aries and Mars at 6 Libra, they would be in opposition. The opposition aspect adds stress between the planets.

Sextile: A space of 60 degrees (+ 4 degrees) between two planets is known as a sextile. If Uranus were at 19 Virgo and the Moon at 17 Cancer, they would be in sextile. This indicates a harmonious blending of planetary energies.

Square: This is a 90-degree angle (+ 8 degrees) between two planets. If the Sun were at 23 Sagittarius and Saturn at 28 Pisces, they would be in a square aspect. The square indicates a definite inharmonious relationship.

Trine: The most beneficial of all the aspects, the trine is formed when two planets are within 120 degrees apart (+ 8 degrees). If Venus were at 2 Taurus and Jupiter at 3 Virgo, they would be trine to one another.

Autumnal equinox: This is another name for the first day of fall, which is also the first degree of Libra each year. It is the moment when daylight and nighttime hours are equal. After the autumnal equinox, the days grow increasingly shorter.

Cusp: This is the space dividing two signs or houses. If you had 29 degrees of Aries on your ascendant, the astrologer would say that your rising sign is on the cusp of Taurus, as this is the sign following the Ram. If you were born on February 18, your Sun could either be in the last degree of Aquarius or the first degree of Pisces. You would then have your Sun on the Aquarius/Pisces cusp and be a person with characteristics of both signs.

Degree: A space amounting to 1/360th of the zodiac circle.

Descendant: The exact degree of the zodiac opposite the ascendant. The descendant is the cusp of the seventh House of your chart and is very much involved with your personal relationships. If, for example, you had Taurus on the descendant, you would most likely be attracted to earthy, loyal, steadfast, and sensual people.

Elements: The signs fall into one of the four following elements, and your nature and character are affected accordingly. Signs of the same or complementary element usually get along very well with each other.

Air: This is the element of communication, and all the air signs like to talk, share, and create relationships. The three air signs are: Gemini, Libra, and Aquarius. The complement to air is fire.

Earth: These are the practical, cautious, common-sense signs of the zodiac: Taurus, Virgo, and Capricorn. The complement to earth is water.

Fire: The fiery signs are assertive, inspirational, and very creative by nature. They are: Aries, Leo, and Sagittarius.

Water: These are the emotional, sensitive, feeling signs of the zodiac: Cancer, Scorpio, and Pisces.

Ephemeris: This is an important tool for an astrologer. It is a book listing all the positions of the planets, the Sun, Moon, and other essential astronomical data used in astrology. In order to construct a horoscope, you must consult an ephemeris to calculate the celestial positions of the planets. In recent years this is most often accomplished through the use of a computer. There are several very fine computerized astrological programs (including the ephemeris) available to the general public that can save you lots of time and energy should you wish to create your own charts.

Houses: As you have read in "The Houses" chapter, the houses comprise the twelve divisions of your natal horoscope. They fall into three primary categories:

Angular: These are the most important of the chart divisions and comprise the first (ascendant), fourth (nadir or I.C.), seventh (descendant), and the tenth (midheaven or M.C.) houses. They indicate your personal qualities and interests and correspond most naturally to the signs Aries, Cancer, Libra, and Capricorn.

Succedent: These houses reveal what your values are and how you use them. They are the second, fifth, eighth, and eleventh divisions of your chart and correspond most naturally to Taurus, Leo, Scorpio, and Aquarius.

Cadent: These are the four houses that deal mostly with the surrounding circumstances of your life and have a great deal to do with your educational background, mental and emotional health, and secondary family members. These houses are the third, sixth, ninth, and twelfth and correspond most naturally to Gemini, Virgo, Sagittarius, and Pisces.

Inner planets: Also called the "personal planets," these are the celestial bodies that orbit between the Sun and Saturn and include these two plus Mercury, Venus, the Moon, Mars, and Jupiter.

Lights: The Sun and the Moon.

Luminaries: Another term for the Lights.

Midheaven: The topmost degree of your natal horoscope. It is also called the "cusp of the tenth House" and indicates your career potential. It also speaks about your father and your relationship with him.

Mutual reception: This is when two planets are in each other's rulership sign. If Jupiter were in Capricorn and Saturn in Sagittarius, these planets would be in mutual reception and very closely linked to each other in your life.

Nadir: The degree of the zodiac exactly opposite your midheaven in your natal chart. The nadir is also the cusp of the fourth House and indicates the nature of your family background, especially your relationship with your mother and your domestic life in general.

Nativity: Another term for the birth chart. Other words and phrases for this important document are natal map and natal horoscope.

Nodes of the Moon: These are the two points in the heavens where the Moon, in its orbit around the Earth, touches the orbit of the Earth around the Sun. Also called the "Dragon's Head and Tail," the positions of these nodes are very important in the interpretation of a natal chart. They indicate where you can make some major moves forward in your life through your associations (North Node) or where, through certain friendships and relationships, you may not succeed (South Node). The positions of these two Nodes of the Moon may be found in an ephemeris.

Orb: This is the extent of influence existing between two planets, or other sensitive points in a horoscope. A trine between two planets has an orb of + 8 degrees. This means that two planets are in a trine aspect if they are between 112 and 128 degrees apart. This is their "orb of influence."

Outer planets: Also called the "higher octave planets," these are Uranus, Neptune, and Pluto.

Progressions: A technique for seeing future possibilities in a person's life and a major tool for astrological forecasting.

Qualities: In addition to being understood by element, the signs are also divided into the following categories:

Cardinal: Also called "motivational" signs, the cardinal signs are highly self-motivated through their creative impulses (Aries), emotions (Cancer), relationships (Libra), and urge for success in the world (Capricorn).

Fixed: These four signs are the most stable (and the most stubborn!) of the zodiac. They express this quality through the use of their personal resources (Taurus), their personality (Leo), their will power (Scorpio), and their ideals and aspirations (Aquarius).

Mutable: Another name for these four signs is "common." They function to connect and communicate through their ideas (Gemini), practical skills (Virgo), knowledge (Sagittarius), and feelings (Pisces).

Retrograde: This occurs when a planet in the heavens appears to be moving backwards. This is an illusion, as retrogradation occurs only when the Earth in its orbit is moving faster than the planet, overtaking this "retrograde planet" as all the spheres move around the Sun.

Rulership: This is the sign or house most closely connected to a given planet. Mars, for example, is the ruler of Aries and the first house. Rulership also applies to people, places, and things that are closely connected to a sign, house, or planet. Food in general is under the rulership of the Moon, health under the rulership of Virgo, France under the rulership of Leo, brothers and sisters under the rulership of the third house, etc.

Solar chart: When the time of birth is unknown, astrologers usually take the degree of the Sun on the day of birth (found in the ephemeris) and use it as the degree of the ascendant. The horoscope is then divided into twelve equal parts using that same degree for each of the house cusps.

Stellium: When four or more planets are in the same sign of the zodiac at the time of birth. This places a tremendous emphasis on the characteristics of that sign in a person's life.

Summer solstice: The longest day of the year, always occurring at the first degree of Cancer.

Synastry: Also known as "chart comparison," this is a technique used by astrologers to understand the compatibility existing between two people.

Table of houses: This is a book listing the degrees of the house cusps of the natal chart for the latitude of the place of birth. This information is always included in a computerized astrological program.

Transits: This represents the current positions of the planets in the heavens at any given time. The transits are another important tool used in astrological forecasting.

Vernal equinox: The first day of spring, when the hours of day and night are equal and after which the days gradually grow longer. The vernal equinox is always at the first degree of Aries of each year.

Winter solstice: This is the shortest day of the year and is always at the first degree of Capricorn of each year.

If this short list of astrological terms sparks your interest, please consult the books listed in the following Recommended Reading and Study Material list for more detailed studies of this fascinating subject.

RECOMMENDED READING AND STUDY MATERIAL

Additional works by Alan Oken:

Alan Oken's Complete Astrology, New York: Bantam Books, 1988.
Soul-Centered Astrology, Freedom, CA: The Crossing Press, 1996.
Your Sun Sign, cassette tape series. Santa Fe, NM: Now Productions.
Your Heart Sign, cassette tape series. Santa Fe, NM: Now Productions.

Other useful sources:

Carter, Charles. *The Principles of Astrology*. Wheaton, IL: The Theosophical Publishing House, 1963.

Heindel, M. *The Message of the Stars*. Oceanside, CA: Rosicrucian Fellowship, 1940.

Hickey, Isabel. *Astrology: A Cosmic Science*. 1970. Privately published. Available through Hickey, 103 Goldencrest Ave., Waltham, MA 02154.

Rudhyar, Dane. *The Astrology of Personality*. New York: Lucis Trust, 1936.

Ruperti, A. *Cycles of Becoming*. Vancouver, WA: CRCS Publications, 1978.

Spiller, Jan. and McCoy, K. *Spiritual Astrology*. New York: Simon and Schuster, 1988.

Wickenburg, J. *A Journey Through the Birth Chart*. Reno, NV: CRCS Publications, 1985.

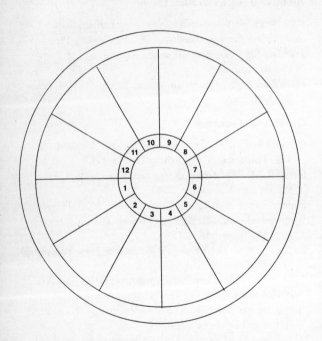

Notes

Chart

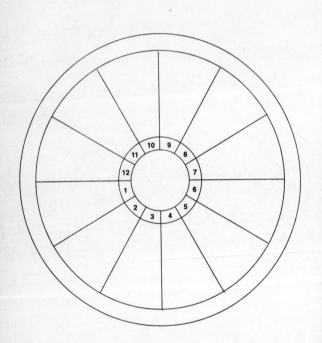

Notes

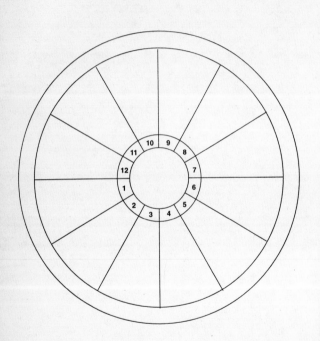

Notes

Other pocket guides from The Crossing Press

Pocket Guide to Ayurvedic Healing
By Candis Cantin Packard
Paper • ISBN 0-89594-764-1

Pocket Guide to Good Food
By Margaret M. Wittenberg
Paper • ISBN 0-89594-747-1

Pocket Herbal Reference Guide
By Debra Nuzzi, Master Herbalist
Paper • ISBN 0-89594-568-1

Pocket Guide to Aromatherapy
By Kathi Keville
Paper • ISBN 0-89594-815-X

Pocket Guide to Naturopathic Medicine
By Judith Boice
Paper • ISBN 0-89594-821-4

Pocket Guide to Numerology
By Alan Oken
Paper • ISBN 0-89594-826-5

Pocket Guide to the Tarot
By Alan Oken
Paper • 0-89594-822-2

For a current catalog of books from The Crossing Press
visit our Web site: **www.crossingpress.com**